THE LIVING
WHITE HOUSE

TEXT BY LONNELLE AIKMAN

Published by the
WHITE HOUSE HISTORICAL ASSOCIATION
with the cooperation of the
NATIONAL GEOGRAPHIC SOCIETY
Washington, D. C.

WHITE HOUSE HISTORICAL ASSOCIATION

THE LIVING WHITE HOUSE
by Lonnelle Aikman

Mary Ann Harrell, *Stylist*
Geraldine Linder, *Illustrations Research*
Margaret B. Klapthor, Curator Emeritus, Division of Political History, National Museum of American History, Smithsonian Institution; and Dr. Richard L. Watson, Jr., Professor Emeritus of History, Duke University, *Text Consultants*

Produced by the National Geographic Society as a public service
Reg Murphy, *President and Chief Executive Officer*
Gilbert M. Grosvenor, *Chairman of the Board*
Nina D. Hoffman, *Senior Vice President*

PREPARED BY THE BOOK DIVISION
William R. Gray, *Vice President and Director*
Charles Kogod, *Assistant Director*
Barbara A. Payne, *Editorial Director*

Jane H. Buxton, *Managing Editor*
Carolinda E. Hill, *Contributing Editor*
Lori Davie Price, *Researcher*
Susan A. Franques, *Contributing Researcher*
Jody Bolt Littlehales, *Art Director*
Suez B. Kehl, *Contributing Art Director*
Elizabeth Schleichert, *Revision Writer*
Elisabeth MacRae-Bobynskyj, *Indexer*
Manufacturing and Quality Management: George V. White, *Director;* Clifton M. Brown III, *Manager*

White House staff members who assisted in preparing this edition: Neel Lattimore, *Press Secretary to the First Lady;* Rex Scouten, *Curator;* Betty C. Monkman, *Associate Curator;* Lydia F. Tederick, *Assistant Curator;* Lori Wiener, *Photo Editor*

OPPOSITE: Beaming with seasonal cheer, President Clinton, the First Lady, and their daughter, Chelsea, pose for a family portrait on the South Portico in December 1994.

COVER: Off to the races: Youngsters at the 1994 White House Easter Egg Roll inch their eggs down the south lawn course toward the finish line under the watchful eyes of volunteers.

THE WHITE HOUSE

PAGE 1: Glowing gas jets turn the White House to gold as guests arrive for a January reception in 1886, during President Grover Cleveland's first term.

PAGES 2-3: President Clinton toasts recipients of the Presidential Arts Medal on October 7, 1993, in the State Dining Room.

PAGE 6: "Nothing is more important to our shared future than the well-being of children," says First Lady Hillary Rodham Clinton, who shares a moment in June 1995 with young guests on the south grounds.

CONTENTS

FOREWORD

FOR YEARS, I HAVE BEEN FASCINATED by the White House. As a child, I loved to gaze at photographs of it, and later, whenever I flew into Washington, as the plane swept low over the Potomac, I would strain for a glimpse of its graceful, stately lines. The President and I are proud to offer this book, *The Living White House*, to you in celebration of the history of this marvelous place and of the families who have lived here.

I have a great sense of humility about all that has happened at the White House over the years. One of the starkest reminders of its past are the burn marks from the fire set by the British during the War of 1812. I get goose bumps every time I see these on the north side of the house and on the South Portico. I frequently get overwhelmed when I walk from room to room and think about all that has gone on here. For instance, when I walk into what is now the Lincoln bedroom, which served as President Lincoln's office, I see the place where he drafted the Emancipation Proclamation. And atop a desk in this room lies the only signed, dated, and titled copy of the Gettysburg Address in Lincoln's hand.

The President and I have felt what an extraordinary privilege it is to live in the White House. The house itself really is majestic—the style of it, the layout, the additions—all have maintained its sense of grandeur without turning it into an imperial palace. It is also the only residence of a head of state anywhere in the world that is open to the public on a regular basis, free of charge. More than a million visitors a year walk into this home and stroll on the grounds. That is a stunning tribute to the continuity of tradition and the strength of our democracy that is unique in world history.

Like many First Ladies, I have enjoyed the opportunity this role has provided to highlight specific issues that have concerned me for a long time. I have grappled with and spoken out about issues affecting children and women, education, and health care—in an effort to broaden people's awareness and to bring about positive changes in these areas.

But equally important to President Clinton and me has been the chance to share our love of the White House with our friends and a wide array of visitors. We hope you will enjoy your own visit now as you delve into the stories that bring the President's House to life here in the tenth edition of *The Living White House*, proudly published by the White House Historical Association and produced by the National Geographic Society.

Hillary Rodham Clinton

7

1

HAIL TO
THE CHIEF

THE WHITE HOUSE is part of every American's national inheritance. As the office and home of the President, it is the one place toward which citizens look for leadership from the man they have chosen to act for all. No other elected official is so directly accountable to them. Their problems are his problems; his home is theirs.

John Adams, the first Chief Executive to live in the White House, once wrote, "People of the United States! You know not half the solicitude of your presidents for your happiness and welfare. . . ."

"I never forget," said President Franklin Delano Roosevelt in one of his famous fireside chats, "that I live in a house owned by all the American people and that I have been given their trust."

The Executive Mansion has been a focal point of government and a barometer of the political, economic, and social state of the nation ever since it was first occupied in 1800, a decade after Congress had set up the country's permanent capital in the fields and forests beside the Potomac River. It has known the tramp and flames of enemy invaders; victory celebrations and economic depressions; high-fashion weddings; and the somber pageantry of state funerals.

Unlike the ornate and monumental palaces of Europe's royal past, the porticoed White House stands today with unpretentious charm amid green and rolling grounds in the heart of Washington. Some visitors may

President Clinton waves before stepping into Marine One in August 1995. The helicopter took Clinton to Andrews Air Force Base, where the presidential jet, Air Force One, waited to fly him to a convention in Charlotte, North Carolina.

think that it still looks "like an English clubhouse," as British novelist Charles Dickens described it after visiting President Tyler in 1841. Separating the mansion from the hustle and bustle of hurrying pedestrians is a high iron fence. A shooting outside the north gate and the bombing of a federal building in Oklahoma City prompted President Clinton to close the two-block section of Pennsylvania Avenue in front of the White House to vehicular traffic on May 20, 1995.

The first four Presidents who lived in the house—John Adams, Thomas Jefferson, James Madison, and James Monroe—earned their credentials for the nation's highest post by serving the cause of American independence and helping to hammer out the Constitution.

George Washington, though "Father of His Country" and "first in the hearts of his countrymen," was the only President who never slept in the White House. He ended his service as Chief Executive and died before the federal government was moved from Philadelphia to the village capital named in his honor.

On a visit to the Federal City, George Washington inspects the unfinished President's House with architect James Hoban. Below, houses top a hill in Georgetown (at left) and line the Potomac River waterfront of Washington in a romantic engraving published in 1801.

E VEN SO, WASHINGTON left the indelible mark of his own dignity and good taste on this 18th-century building with its magnificent view. He selected its site and gave his prestigious approval to the simple, harmonious design for the mansion submitted by Irish architect James Hoban in a democratically open competition.

From the beginning the "President's House"—the name Washington preferred—was destined to be a stage for events that marked the progress of the nation from fewer than a score of states stretched along the Atlantic seaboard to a preeminent world power reaching into the Pacific Ocean. Here President Jefferson devised a plan, soon after his inauguration, to purchase the French-owned port of New Orleans and thus keep the Mississippi River outlet open to American trade.

The move would have far-reaching consequences, which Jefferson was quick to appreciate after Napoleon suddenly offered to sell not only the port but also the entire wilderness empire reaching from the Mississippi River deep into the West.

Known as the Louisiana Purchase, the treaty was negotiated with Napoleon's representatives in Paris by Jefferson's special envoy, James Monroe, and the American minister, Robert R. Livingston. Its ratification by Congress—despite Jefferson's own doubts about the deal's constitutionality—virtually doubled the territory of the young Republic at a bargain price of $15,000,000. It also underscored the practical need for the Lewis and Clark expedition that Jefferson had already launched to explore the region.

To the President's House in 1829 came tough, flamboyant Andrew Jackson. "Old Hickory" was the first man to reach the top executive office from the open frontier beyond the Appalachians. His overwhelming presidential victory in 1828 clearly demonstrated the new political power of a growing and more democratically based electorate, and it alerted the aristocratic statesmen of the East to a fact of life: Henceforth

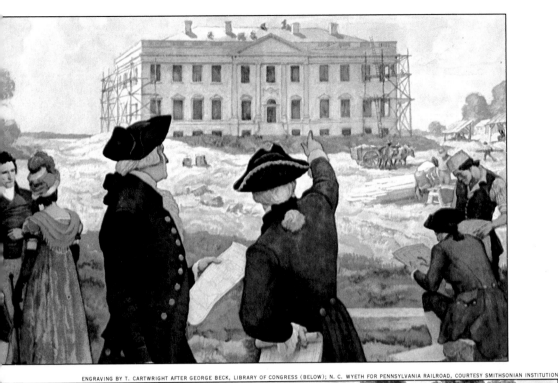

ENGRAVING BY T. CARTWRIGHT AFTER GEORGE BECK, LIBRARY OF CONGRESS (BELOW); N. C. WYETH FOR PENNSYLVANIA RAILROAD, COURTESY SMITHSONIAN INSTITUTION national leadership must be shared with the people of the West.

During his first few years in the presidential saddle, Jackson rode head on into a furious controversy growing out of intense sectional rivalry between northern and southern states, and foreshadowing the eventual bloody test of the Union's very survival.

The long dispute came to a climax in 1832 when South Carolina nullified a federal tariff on foreign imports, levied to aid northern manufacturers. From the White House the President issued a warning proclamation. In his statement Jackson called South Carolina's claim of states' rights, coupled with threats of secession, a "fatal doctrine" whose success would mean "our present happy Constitution was formed . . . in vain. . . ."

Putting muscle behind his words, he sent ships to command the port of Charleston and made it clear that he would call out federal troops if necessary. Armed confrontation seemed imminent, but Jackson's firm stand, followed by Congress's reduction of import taxes in general, eased tension. The crisis passed.

Three decades later, Abraham Lincoln bore the burdens and heartbreak of the "irrepressible conflict" of the Civil War in the vortex of the struggle—the White House. Through bitter military reverses and petty partisan politics—in the face of cruel criticism and cartoons picturing him as a clown and a devil—he held together the frayed bonds of union until the nation could again be united.

"I think of Lincoln, shambling, homely, with his strong, sad, deeply furrowed face, all the time," Theodore Roosevelt wrote a friend after he, too, came to live and work in this house of historic memory. "I see him in the different rooms and in the halls . . . he is to me infinitely the most real of the dead Presidents."

But the fascination the building holds for most Americans has its roots in more than just association with the great men who helped create the United States.

T HE WHITE HOUSE, whose long-popular name was not officially inscribed on the presidential letterhead until Theodore Roosevelt's time, stands as a living symbol of the nation's power and prestige. The office of the Chief Executive is the keystone of the government. Flanked by the Congress and the Supreme Court, it is the central theater of action in which national gains are won and defended.

In a world of dire emergencies and instant communications, the White House has become a focal point of the fierce, incessant searchlight of global attention. To meet the demand to know what goes on here, some 100 reporters and photographers—from newspapers, magazines, television, and radio—regularly cover activities of the President and First Lady. Nearly 2,000 others have credentials and attend special events, such as visits of foreign officials.

Since World War II, an ever lengthening procession of foreign leaders has come to 1600 Pennsylvania Avenue to confer on global problems.

Abigail Adams, welcomed at right by her husband, John, arrives at the still-unfinished White House. The couple lived here only four months before Adams's term expired in 1801. Above, granddaughter Susanna helps supervise as a servant hangs wash in the East Room.

PAINTING BY GORDON PHILLIPS, 1966 (ABOVE); DRAWING BY LOUIS S. GLANZMAN, 1970

Thomas Jefferson observes a black-billed magpie and a prairie dog, brought 4,000 miles in 1805 from the winter camp of the Lewis and Clark Expedition. He sent them to Charles Willson Peale of Philadelphia, who had established a museum in Independence Hall. Thanking Jefferson, Peale wrote: ". . . every thing that comes from Louisiana must be interresting to the Public."

Usually dignitaries are also formally entertained at the White House, and an invitation to attend such a function is highly coveted. Certainly a state dinner to honor a visiting head of government or a reigning monarch is one of the most glamorous of White House affairs.

At the white-columned North Entrance, the President and his wife greet their guests of honor and escort them to the second-floor Yellow Oval Room. There they meet with other top-ranking guests, such as the Secretary of State. Meantime, a hundred or so other guests are arriving at the East Entrance. Leaving their wraps in the East Wing, they ascend the marble stairway to the State Floor.

There, they are presented with cards explaining seating arrangements and conducted to the East Room by social aides, officers chosen from the Armed Forces. On their way, guests walk across the Entrance Hall, where the red-coated Marine Band—"The President's Own" since 1801—is playing a lively popular tune. As they enter the room, another social aide announces each new arrival.

Suddenly the aides snap to attention and the music changes to the stirring strains of a march. The President and his wife, with their guests of honor, are descending the grand stairway from the family floor. At the foot of the steps, the group pauses for official photographs. Then, to the roll of drums in the familiar "Ruffles and Flourishes" salute, followed by the triumphant march "Hail to the Chief," the President and his party form the official receiving line.

The host and hostess greet the assembled guests in protocol order and present them to the honored visitors. Finally, the President and First Lady escort the visitors to the State Dining Room, and the other guests follow in turn.

The public does not have to wait long to learn details of the dinner. Late-night television newscasts and next-day newspapers often carry pictures and stories on the guests, menu, and entertainment. To obtain such information and to add firsthand descriptions to their coverage, a few White House reporters have long been permitted to attend the after-dinner entertainment and to chat with the guests.

As another aid to the news media, President Johnson had an electronic system installed so that reporters assembled in another room could hear the traditional toasts exchanged by the two heads of state. More recently, some foreign leaders have arranged for video coverage of the dinners for live broadcast or later use in their home countries.

FROM 1993 THROUGH 1996, Bill Clinton was host at the White House for 12 state visits. His guests came from around the globe: from Europe, Africa, and Asia; from North and South America. Among the honored guests were France's President Jacques Chirac, Ireland's President Mary Robinson, South Africa's President Nelson Mandela, and Mexico's President Ernesto Zedillo. President Clinton has consulted with more than 193 world leaders, including 95 presidents, 6 kings, 5 queens, 77 prime ministers, 2 chancellors, and numerous ambassadors and foreign ministers.

In another and more intimate aspect, the White House occupies a unique place in American life. As the home of presidential families for nearly 200 years, it has represented, by democratic extension, the homes and families of all Americans.

Since the early federal period of John and Abigail Adams, this "First Home" has mirrored America's everyday domestic fashions and attitudes, household decor, furnishings and utensils, in ways that would have been unthinkable to the followers of social and political traditions practiced in Europe's great state residences.

More than that, the personal and family life in the White House has given to this center of national power and influence a warm, human note of common experience and understanding.

President and Mrs. John Adams, for instance, were far from happy in November 1800 when the time came to move into the damp and incomplete Executive Mansion being readied in the raw little capital. Only four months remained of Adams's single term, and Mrs. Adams was dismayed at the condition of their temporary home.

The house was "made habitable," she wrote her daughter in Massachusetts, but the main stairs were not yet up, not a single apartment had been finished, and bells for summoning the servants were "wholly wanting to assist us in this great castle."

Abigail's rheumatism came back, too, in the chill caused by a scarcity of logs for the many fireplaces. "Shiver, shiver," she complained, ". . . surrounded with forests, can you believe that wood is not to be had, because people cannot be found to cut and cart it!"

The most famous housekeeping problem Mrs. Adams faced, however, still makes an amusing subject for conversation at White House parties. Since there was, she said, "not the least fence, yard, or other convenience" available outside, she had a servant hang the presidential laundry to dry in the huge, unfinished East Room, destined to become the most elegant of the state chambers used in entertaining.

Beginning with John Adams, whose personal discomfort in the new White House was matched only by the political vicissitudes of his outgoing administration, each succeeding President has led two lives while in office—his own and his country's.

Thomas Jefferson, a scholar and a gentleman, confounded Federalists who predicted that his belief in equality would bring disorder and destruction. Instead, he maintained an atmosphere of personal moderation and a social style of fine living and intellectual interests that belied the crude surroundings of the wilderness capital.

To relax from the heavy responsibilities of leadership in a young republic starting out in a world of hostile monarchies, the long-widowed President turned to hobbies he had enjoyed at his Monticello home. He played his fiddle, experimented with familiar and rare plants, and taught his pet mockingbird to peck food from his lips and to hop up the stairs after him.

The White House reflected the quiet happiness of James and Dolley Madison and the generous hospitality presided over by the genial Dolley before they were burned out of the mansion in the War of 1812.

Washington Irving, after attending one of Mrs. Madison's popular Wednesday-evening receptions, described her as "a fine, portly, buxom dame" and "poor Jemmey . . . a withered little apple-John." Others pointed out the couple's mutual devotion and admiration. Dolley once wrote that the sensitive, studious President was her "darling little husband." He said a conversation with her always brought a bright story and a good laugh, as refreshing as a long walk in the park.

AMONG MORE RECENT PRESIDENTS, Woodrow Wilson often appeared to outsiders as a perfect example of the austere, erudite professor. Yet within his close and affectionate family before the death of his wife, Ellen, he was a jaunty, fun-loving man, fond of group singing, impersonations, and limericks.

When he married again, after a period of deep despondency, President Wilson found with his second wife, Edith, a renewal of happiness he had never expected to know again. Without her "love and care . . . I

Near the end of the War of 1812, fire set by British troops roars through the White House, August 24, 1814. Dolley Madison (diorama) salvaged what she could, including the Gilbert Stuart portrait of George Washington (far right).

don't believe he could live," Mrs. Wilson's social secretary, Edith Ben-ham, wrote in the dark days after the strain of his stubborn but futile League of Nations campaign had left him a paralyzed, broken man.

The Dwight D. Eisenhowers established at the White House the most permanent home they had known during the far-ranging career of the popular general with the broad smile. "I have seen my grandchildren growing up in these historic rooms," Mrs. Eisenhower wrote. "Here my son and daughter-in-law have shared our family evenings."

Life with the Carters reflected the easy atmosphere found in many small southern towns, such as their native Plains, Georgia. A story that made the capital rounds early in 1977 revealed something of their ways. Picking up a telephone soon after she arrived at the White House, Mrs. Carter asked to be connected with Jimmy. "Jimmy who?" came the response from the operator.

President Reagan and his wife, Nancy, introduced a bit of Califor-nia's casual lifestyle, plus a touch of elegance, to the mansion. The Bushes created a warm family atmosphere and entertained in a traditional style reminiscent of their years of diplomatic service and their lives in Texas and on the Maine coast.

President Clinton and his wife, Hillary, bring an energetic style to the White House that is marked by a combination of traditional, formal, and casual entertaining, with an emphasis on making their guests feel comfortable and at home.

President Andrew Jackson salutes—and strengthens—the Federal Union, threatened by talk of secession. At a Washington banquet on April 30, 1830, backers of a plan to nullify a Federal tariff opposed by South Carolina gave 24 toasts full of states' rights ideas. Jackson's simple reply rallied public opinion to his position: "Our Federal Union— It must be preserved."

OVER THE YEARS, the public image projected by every President and his family has been part fiction and part reality, part per-sonal and part official. Until 1902, when Theodore Roosevelt built the West Wing to separate his office from his living quarters, all fam-ilies shared the Executive Mansion with the public, which was freely admitted to ask favors, to seek interviews with the President, or just to shake his hand.

When Herbert Hoover and his wife, Lou, invited all comers to the traditional New Year's Day reception in 1930, 6,000 people appeared. By 1932, the annual open house and handshaking had become such an ordeal that the Hoovers decided to be out of town the following year. The cus-tom was never revived.

The President's House, as the people's property, has remained open in selected areas under regulations permitting as much inspection as pos-sible without interfering with the family's privacy or with official func-tions. From Tuesday through Saturday, sightseers—more than a million annually—make their way from the new Visitors Center to the White House, lining up by the iron fence enclosing the 18-acre estate.

Surging through the East Gate, they enter the East Wing, then walk through the Ground Floor Corridor and up a marble stairway to find an astonishing, colorful spectacle. Here, five state rooms, one opening into another, spread a brilliant pageant, from the white-and-gold East Room, through the Green, Blue, and Red Rooms, to the State Dining Room.

Furnished in late 18th- and early 19th-century styles—original pieces and faithful reproductions—these rooms are much like stage sets, with portraits of past Presidents and First Ladies enhancing the scene. Life-size paintings of George and Martha Washington dominate the capacious East Room. The Gilbert Stuart likeness of the first President, obtained in 1800, is the oldest remaining possession of the house.

It was this priceless portrait that Dolley Madison saved when she fled before British troops approaching Washington during the War of 1812. President Madison had joined the defending forces in Maryland. Mrs. Madison, in a letter to her sister, explained how she saved the painting. "Our kind friend, Mr. Carroll, has come to hasten my departure," she wrote, "and is in a very bad humor with me, because I insist on waiting until the large picture of Gen. Washington is secured, and it requires to be unscrewed from the wall. This process was found too tedious…I have ordered the frame to be broken and the canvas taken out; it is done."

Many other portraits of those whose lives are forever interwoven with memories of this building hang in the state rooms. Their attire, from knee breeches and hoopskirts to modern dress, recalls the many eras the house has known, as Presidents moved in to shape and be shaped by events, and to leave on the American character the imprint of their philosophy and words. Jefferson wrote, ". . . our liberty can never be safe but in the hands of the people themselves." Lincoln said, "with malice toward none . . ." and showed compassion that might have helped heal the wounds after the fratricidal war if he had survived.

"Speak softly and carry a big stick," was a favorite motto of "Teddy" Roosevelt, who launched the building of the Panama Canal, won a formidable reputation for "trust-busting," and sent 16 battleships of the United States Navy on parade around the world.

A long list of memorable phrases emerged during the White House years of Franklin D. Roosevelt, the only President elected to four terms. Best remembered perhaps are the "New Deal," "economic royalists," "arsenal of democracy," and "the Four Freedoms."

Considered as a group, the 41 men who have taken on their country's

Abraham Lincoln, tallest man present, welcomes guests near a White House doorway during a "Grand Reception" in January 1862. Mrs. Lincoln nods a chilly greeting to Secretary of the Treasury Salmon P. Chase and his daughter, Kate (center). Kate had earned Mrs. Lincoln's dislike by promoting her father's campaign for the Presidency.

toughest assignment reflect the geographic and cultural diversity that is the hallmark and strength of this nation. Virginia, "Mother of Presidents," claims eight as native sons. Ohio has contributed seven; Massachusetts and New York, four each; North Carolina, Texas, and Vermont, two apiece. Arkansas, California, Illinois, Iowa, Kentucky, Missouri, Nebraska, New Hampshire, New Jersey, Pennsylvania, South Carolina, and Georgia have each produced one President.

Together, the lives of these varied leaders support the democratic proposition that every American, however humble in origin, has a chance to reach the highest position in the land. Abraham Lincoln was born in a log cabin, as were several other Chief Executives. The exact number is uncertain because of confused birth records, but the claim of humble origins, authentic or not, had potent political appeal in frontier days.

The rollicking campaign of William Henry Harrison rolled to success

Troops of the Bucktail Brigade—Company K of the 150th Regiment of Pennsylvania Volunteers—seek the shade for

a cribbage game. The Bucktails—named for snippets of fur on their caps—guarded Lincoln during the Civil War.

in 1840 on a bandwagon bearing twin symbols of a log cabin and a barrel of hard cider, despite the fact that Harrison was not born in a log cabin but was a scion of Virginia aristocracy and had no special taste for cider.

As to education, Lincoln was self-taught, and Jackson's lack of academic learning was sometimes cited to embarrass him, while the Adamses—both father and son—were Harvard graduates, experienced in the diplomatic and social circles of Europe.

Andrew Johnson, who learned to read and write with his wife's help, was a tailor before he entered politics. Franklin D. Roosevelt came from a rich and patrician family of New York. John F. Kennedy, descendant of Irish immigrants, inherited drive and fortune from a father whose business acumen brought his family millions; and Richard M. Nixon was reared in Whittier, California, the second of five sons, in a modest Quaker home. Gerald R. Ford grew up in Grand Rapids, Michigan, as the adopted son of a devoted stepfather—a small businessman struggling to survive the Great Depression of the thirties.

Jimmy Carter graduated from the Naval Academy in 1946 but gave up a seagoing career to take over the family peanut farm after his father's death. Elected to the Georgia Senate, he went on to serve as governor before becoming President. Ronald Reagan was the first professional actor to achieve America's highest political rank. Earlier, Reagan worked as a radio sportscaster, served as a captain in the U.S. Army Air Corps, and was twice elected governor of California.

George Bush, a Yale graduate, began his political career as a congressman from Texas. He held several high-level positions, including those of U.S. Ambassador to the United Nations and Director of the Central Intelligence Agency. He was the first sitting Vice President in more than 150 years to be elected President.

William Jefferson Clinton was born and raised in Arkansas, graduated from Georgetown University, and studied at Oxford University as a Rhodes scholar. After receiving his law degree from Yale University in 1973, he taught law at the University of Arkansas. The following year he was defeated in his campaign for Congress. In 1975 he married Hillary Rodham, who became not just his wife, but his political partner as well.

Amicable transfer of power, hallmark of the American system, keeps the government running smoothly. At Woodrow Wilson's inauguration in 1913, he and President Taft ride from the White House to the Capitol in a four-horse victoria. Above, on their last morning in the mansion in 1961, President and Mrs. Eisenhower bid farewell to staff members.

He was elected attorney general of Arkansas and went on to become the governor. At age 46, Clinton became the first President elected from the "baby boom" generation.

Eleven Presidents were former generals—including George Washington and Dwight Eisenhower. Warren Harding was a newspaper publisher; Herbert Hoover was an engineer. Several were teachers or college professors. At least 20 practiced law early in their careers; many served as state officials, Members of Congress, and Cabinet officers.

Eight Vice Presidents rose to the Presidency on the death of incumbents; four of these—Theodore Roosevelt, Calvin Coolidge, Harry S. Truman, and Lyndon Johnson—went on to win another term on their own. Gerald R. Ford was the only Vice President to attain the office by the resignation of a Chief Executive. He replaced Richard M. Nixon, who left under threat of impeachment by Congress.

Another novel event in presidential history occurred when William Howard Taft, following his defeat for a second term in 1912, was appointed by President Harding to be Chief Justice of the United

President Nixon faces an array of cameras as he welcomes students on the White House lawn. The early-day amateur photographer above, with one of the first box cameras, took pictures of the Easter egg rolling on the grounds in 1889.

States—the only man ever to serve in both high posts. Of the two, Taft preferred heading the Supreme Court. "I don't remember that I was ever President," he once remarked happily.

Others reacted in different ways to the executive burdens. "I enjoy being President," Theodore Roosevelt wrote to his son Kermit, "and I like to do the work and have my hand on the lever." John Quincy Adams remembered his years at the White House as "the four most miserable" of his life. Truman called the mansion "a great white prison."

"What is there in this place," cried James A. Garfield, who was hounded by office seekers, and who would finally be murdered by one, "that a man should ever want to get in it."

Yet there has never been a shortage of candidates for the position that Jefferson described as "a splendid misery," and Jackson found to be "dignified slavery." Coolidge dryly commented, when warned of the dangerous condition of the White House roof, that he presumed there were plenty of others willing to risk living under it.

In view of the frantic nature of many election campaigns, it is amazing that there has never been an interruption in the lawful exchange of masters at 1600 Pennsylvania Avenue. The nearest approach to such disruption occurred in 1877, after Rutherford B. Hayes lost the popular vote to his rival, Samuel J. Tilden, and neither candidate won the necessary majority in the Electoral College. With the opposing parties deadlocked, an Electoral Commission chosen by Congress decided in favor of Hayes. But Tilden's followers challenged the decision.

Because of the bitter dispute and because March 4, then the legal Inauguration Day, fell on Sunday, Hayes took the oath of office in a private White House ceremony on March 3 while attending a dinner given by outgoing President Ulysses S. Grant.

Few of the dinner guests were aware of the event when President Grant quietly led the other principals into the Red Room, where Hayes was secretly sworn in by Chief Justice Morrison R. Waite. The formal inauguration took place peacefully at the Capitol on Monday, March 5.

However placid the transfer of leadership, each new President inherited heavier and more complex duties and responsibilities as the nation grew from some five million people in 1800 to some two hundred and sixty million in 1990. Behind the stately pillars of the Executive Residence, as in the inconspicuous East and West Wings where most official business goes on, many staff members help their chief meet his obligations, great and small. Their tasks include gathering information and receiving visitors, handling mail and documents, carrying on domestic routines, and preparing for a constant round of social and other activities.

EVEN THE MUSEUM-LIKE STATE ROOMS are forever in use when not on public display. Though the press records the official events held in these historic rooms, few people—other than the ones responsible for providing facilities and food—realize the extent and variety of the succession of social and working functions.

State dinners presided over by President and Mrs. Clinton have honored Emperor Akihito and Empress Michiko of Japan, President Nelson Mandela of South Africa, King Hassan II of Morocco, German Chancellor Helmut Kohl, Ukrainian President Leonid Kuchma, President Fernando Henrique Cardoso of Brazil, President Kim Young Sam of South Korea, and President Ernesto Zedillo of Mexico. Other official visitors have included King Hussein of Jordan and Israeli Prime Minister Yitzhak Rabin, Canadian Prime Minister Brian Mulroney, Great Britain's John Major, and French Presidents François Mitterand and Jacques Chirac.

On October 4, 1994, at a historic dinner in the East Room honoring Nelson Mandela, President Clinton toasted the South African President by quoting from a letter Mandela had written during his 27-year imprisonment, "There are few misfortunes in this world you cannot turn into personal triumphs if you have the iron will and necessary skills." Clinton then turned to his guest and noted, "President Mandela, you have shown us the iron will and the necessary skills."

The East Room, where most press conferences are held, has been the setting not only for the occasional dinner, but also for entertainment on numerous occasions. For instance, a local German chorus serenaded guests over cocktails here in February 1995 before a state dinner honoring Chancellor Helmut Kohl. After the meal, everyone gathered in the East Room again to hear a performance by singer Tony Bennett.

The State Dining Room provides an elegant setting for formal dinners. At smaller, less formal dinners, the Clintons often invite guests upstairs for before-dinner refreshments in the Yellow Oval Room or on the Truman Balcony. The party then descends to the Blue Room or the State Dining Room for dinner.

Receptions have been held in each of the state rooms. In their first two years in office, the Clintons entertained 214,000 guests at a variety of events. Among those so honored were musicians, business people, actors, journalists, politicians, and foundation heads.

"Entertaining is something that gives us a lot of pleasure because my husband loves to have people around," commented Mrs. Clinton. "He loves music, good food, and good conversation and so do I," she added.

Whether they come for parties, work, or sightseeing, visitors find inscribed on the mantel of the State Dining Room a benediction and an expression of hope from the earliest days of the Republic. The words were taken from a letter written by John Adams on his second night in the building. Franklin Roosevelt had them cut into the mantel face so that all who passed might see:

"I Pray Heaven to Bestow
The Best of Blessings on
THIS HOUSE
and on All that shall hereafter
Inhabit it. May none but Honest
and Wise Men ever rule under This Roof."

A gathering of notables: Former Presidents Ford, Bush, and Carter share a relaxed moment with President Clinton in September 1993. In town for the signing of a peace agreement between Israel and the Palestine Liberation Organization, the former Chief Executives joined the President for an informal breakfast at the White House.

2

WHERE HOSPITALITY MAKES HISTORY

AT NO OTHER TIME OF YEAR is the White House more beautiful and festive than during the Christmas season, when it is decked with holiday finery. During the month of December 1993, some 150,000 visitors strolled through the public rooms, enjoying the Yuletide decorations. The dazzling display included a giant mistletoe ball in the Entrance Hall, doors and hallways adorned with bows and wreaths, and 22 Christmas trees and numerous garlands sparkling with 27,035 tiny white lights.

The 18½-foot Fraser fir in the Blue Room, the official White House tree, and five other trees were decorated with American craft ornaments of fiber, ceramic, glass, wood, and metal. Made by 3,000 artisans, the ornaments were displayed in honor of the Year of the American Craft. Some of them showed the President as a jack-in-the-box with a saxophone, and President and Mrs. Clinton, Chelsea, and Socks as angels. Beneath the official tree lay a skirt fashioned by American quilters, with squares representing the 50 states and U.S. territories.

Visitors to the State Dining Room could admire the 50-inch-long gingerbread house painstakingly crafted by pastry chef Roland Mesnier and his assistant, Franette McCulloch. It was a fanciful rendering of the White House as the "House of Socks," with 22 miniature versions of the First Cat in various poses, such as pulling Santa's sleigh.

As the focal point of the East Room, six large blue spruce trees were

The Clintons welcome President Kim Young Sam and Kim Myoung Soon of South Korea for a state dinner in July 1995. By protocol, the President and First Lady greet official guests here at the North Portico for such functions.

Dancing at his son's wedding, February 25, 1828, John Quincy Adams steps to a lively Virginia reel with the bride, the former Mary Catherine Hellen. John— the only White House bridegroom among Presidents' sons—talks with his mother (below at left). The officiating clergyman, Dr. William Hawley, stands third from right against the wall. Eight years earlier, on March 9, 1820, he had presided at the wedding of Maria Hester Monroe (left), the first President's daughter to be wed in the White House. She married her cousin, Samuel Laurence Gouverneur, in a private ceremony. Officials and social leaders paid "visits of congratulations" at two evening receptions.

adorned with burgundy and gold ribbons and gleaming gold glass balls. Handcrafted ornaments were displayed amid greenery on mantels and tables. Poinsettias and topiary trees added to the festive decor. In addition to the daytime tours, visitors could go through the state rooms on designated evenings, their way lighted by the flickering glow of candles. A variety of musical groups provided holiday entertainment for visitors.

At other times of the year, the White House showcases a variety of entertainment. President and Mrs. Clinton have continued the series of concerts titled *In Performance at the White House*, initiated by the Carters and broadcast over public television. Mrs. Carter explained that the idea for this program "came about because Jimmy and I knew there were so many people who had never been to the White House....We wanted all of America to enjoy the White House as we did."

The Clintons brought in renowned musicians Wynton Marsalis and Herbie Hancock for a concert on the south lawn celebrating the 40th anniversary of the Newport Jazz Festival in June 1993. A year later, Aretha Franklin and Lou Rawls performed in the Rose Garden. Another event on the south lawn, in May 1995, featured the women of country music, including Kathy Mattea and Alison Krauss.

WHATEVER THEIR PERSONAL STYLE, no President and his wife can ever forget that they act as the nation's official host and hostess. Recognizing this, John and Abigail Adams required guests to show the kind of deference to the new Republic that subjects accorded rulers of monarchies abroad. During their short stay in the village capital, the Adamses practiced the formal court etiquette that had been adopted for a similar reason by President and Mrs. Washington in New York and Philadelphia.

In the upstairs oval room, hung with crimson draperies, Mrs. Adams remained regally seated to greet the town's leading citizens and foreign diplomats who attended the President's weekly levees, or receptions. By her side, dressed in black velvet coat and knee breeches, silver buckles and lace, John Adams bowed solemnly to arrivals, who then took designated seats around the wall.

Such formality went out the window when Thomas Jefferson became President. He emphasized, instead, his cherished ideals of equality and democracy. In his words, he "buried...levees, birthdays, royal parades," and replaced them with two main White House receptions, which were open to all, on New Year's Day and the Fourth of July.

Jefferson entertained Jérôme Bonaparte, Napoleon's youngest brother and the future king of Westphalia, after that impetuous young man married the Baltimore belle, Betsy Patterson. Jefferson once invited his butcher to dinner. The man brought his son, explaining that the boy

Celebrating newfound political power, common folk unleash a fury of admiration ▷
for President Andrew Jackson during his inaugural reception in the White House. "Old Hickory" quietly escaped the mob and spent the night at a hotel.

could use the place left by a guest who was ill. And the President made both feel welcome among the distinguished company.

His dislike for ceremony, however, only highlighted Jefferson's good manners and excellent taste. He served the finest wines and hired a French chef to prepare the most exotic foods. Around his small, informal table, he assembled charming women and the wittiest, most knowledgeable men to be found in the city or coming from abroad to visit the strange young capital.

In learning and accomplishments, Jefferson himself was unique. His interests ranged from music and history to farming, astronomy, anthropology, and architecture. And it was this erudition that President John F. Kennedy referred to in his famous toast at a 1962 dinner honoring Nobel Prize winners. His guests, said Kennedy, made up "the most extraordinary collection of talent, of human knowledge, that has ever been gathered together at the White House, with the possible exception of when Thomas Jefferson dined alone."

P RESIDENT JEFFERSON replaced the custom of bowing with the more democratic practice of shaking hands. The greeting proved so popular that no successor could abandon it, despite the painful pressure from thousands of hands embracing the privilege.

Slight James K. Polk, once described as the "merest tangible fraction of a President," found a way to avoid a painful grip. "When I observed a strong man approaching," he said, "I generally took advantage of him by being a little quicker…seizing him by the top of his fingers, giving him a hearty shake…."

Lincoln performed the task, in the words of an observer, "as though…splitting rails as of yore." On January 1, 1863, before signing the Emancipation Proclamation, he shook hands for three hours at the usual New Year's reception. Upstairs in his Cabinet room, he spread the official copy on the table, dipped his pen in ink, and paused.

"I never…felt more certain that I was doing right…," he said, looking at Secretary of State William H. Seward. "But…my arm is stiff and numb…if they find my hand trembled, they will say, 'he had some compunctions.' But, any way, it is going to be done!" Then, slowly and carefully, Abraham Lincoln wrote the bold signature that appears at the end of the document.

Besides shaking hands with the public at special events, most Presidents regularly made themselves available for the ritual as recently as the time of Calvin Coolidge. White House doors were then opened for the purpose daily, just before lunch. Rather surprisingly, the taciturn New Englander thoroughly enjoyed the contact.

"On one occasion I shook hands with nineteen hundred in thirty-four minutes…," Coolidge recalled in his autobiography. "Instead of a burden, it was a pleasure and a relief to meet people in that way and listen to their greeting, which was often a benediction."

No one ever took more delight in receiving people and making them

First envoys from Imperial Japan bow to President Buchanan and his Cabinet on May 17, 1860. Visiting to exchange ratifications of a commercial treaty, the Japanese presented their documents in a box earlier borne ceremoniously along Pennsylvania Avenue.

welcome than did vivacious Dolley Madison. Even before she became First Lady, she sometimes served as official hostess for the widowed Jefferson while James Madison was Secretary of State.

After she moved into the mansion in 1809, Dolley made the President's House the rallying point of Washington's fast-burgeoning social life. In the "blazing splendor" of her drawing room, as Washington Irving described it, were gathered, said another guest, "all these whom fashion, fame, beauty, wealth or talents, have render'd celebrated."

While the "great little Madison" met with his Cabinet, Dolley often entertained the wives at "dove parties." Taking no sides in political disputes of the day, she was cordial to Federalist and Republican leaders alike. To callers in general, she served refreshments of seedcake and hot bouillon in winter, punch in summer.

Perhaps compensating for the subdued dress of her Quaker girlhood, statuesque Dolley Madison arrayed herself in rich silks and satins and accentuated her height with magnificent turbans, sometimes decked with ostrich plumes. Yet so obvious was her honest friendliness that everyone found her appealing, notwithstanding her exaggerated dress

President Lincoln towers over his guest, Prince Napoleon (wearing sash), as Secretary of State William H. Seward cheerfully talks of victory only two weeks after the Union defeat at Bull Run, July 21, 1861. Beyond a flag-crowned Marine Band pavilion rises the uncompleted Washington Monument.

and mannerisms. "'Tis here the woman who adorns the dress," said a contemporary commentator; "…in her hands the snuff-box seems only a gracious implement…."

In 1812 Mrs. Madison arranged the first nuptials held at the White House—the wedding of her handsome widowed sister, Lucy Payne Washington, to "the estimable & amiable" Supreme Court Justice, Thomas Todd. Even then, according to one observer, dashing Dolley innocently held the spotlight, "looking every inch the queen."

Then suddenly, brutally, the mansion's "Golden Age," as some called the Madison era of entertaining, came to an end. The War of 1812 had broken out five months before Madison's reelection. It dragged on, mostly in sea engagements far from Washington, until the electrifying news struck the capital on a hot August 23, 1814, that the British had landed troops in Maryland. Gathering members of his Cabinet, President Madison galloped off early the next day to join the American forces near Bladensburg, Maryland.

As the battle began, valiant little "Jemmy" sat astride a horse within sight of the front line, while British rockets exploded near him.

FRANK LESLIE'S ILLUSTRATED NEWSPAPER, LIBRARY OF CONGRESS, TINTED BY P. HALL BAGLIE

Meantime, Mrs. Madison remained at the White House, watching through a spyglass for her husband to return, "ready at a moment's warning to enter my carriage and leave the city," as she wrote her sister in an hour-by-hour letter.

"I am still here within sound of the cannon!" she added at three in the afternoon. "Two messengers covered with dust, come to bid me fly; but I wait for him." Friends finally persuaded Dolley to leave and escorted her across the Potomac into Virginia, where Mrs. Madison eventually would join the President. Her flight came none too soon.

Having scattered the Bladensburg defenders, the British troops marched into Washington that evening and put the torch to the White House, the Capitol, and other public buildings. A torrential thunderstorm saved the city from devastating destruction, but the Executive Mansion was reduced to a blackened, burned-out shell. Reconstruction took three years. During the remainder of Madison's Administration, the couple lived in rented houses, where the incomparable Dolley held court, and the President conducted executive affairs in an atmosphere of renewed confidence following the country's second confrontation with the British.

When James Monroe and his family moved into the rebuilt White House in the fall of 1817, its exterior had been painted a gleaming white. Handsomely restored inside, it contained elegantly carved and gilded furniture and decorative objects, many of them ordered by Monroe from France. Nor were the appearances deceptive. The new facade and furnishings marked a return to the pomp and protocol of earlier days.

Guests at the first New Year's reception had a preview of the changed rules when foreign diplomats were greeted with elaborate protocol before the public was admitted. From then on, Monroe insisted, as had Washington and Adams, that respect be shown the United States by placing foreign ministers "upon much the same footing…of form and ceremony" as that required of American ministers at European courts. This meant that diplomats would come to the White House only by invitation, or after requesting a formal audience with the President.

First Lady Elizabeth Monroe adopted a chillier social tone. She refused to continue the exhausting custom of making first calls, or even returning them. Eliza Hay, the Monroes' married daughter who lived in the White House with her husband, carried on her own feud with Diplomatic Corps wives over the etiquette of paying calls.

THE DRASTIC CHANGE from the Madisons' warmth and accessibility alienated Washington's social leaders. They retaliated by boycotting the Monroes' "at homes."

"The drawing-room of the President was opened last night to a 'beggarly row of empty chairs,'" wrote Mrs. William Winston Seaton, wife of a prominent Washington newspaper editor. "Only five females attended, three of whom were foreigners."

More steam came from the teapot tempest when plans were announced for the wedding of pretty little Maria Monroe, not yet 17, to her cousin and her father's secretary, Samuel Laurence Gouverneur. The first White House marriage of a President's daughter would be private, the family decreed. Foreign diplomats were pointedly advised "to take no notice" of the event.

Afterward Mrs. Seaton commented briefly, "The New York style was adopted…. Only the attendants, the relations, and a few old friends of the bride and groom witnessed the ceremony…."

In long-range social prestige, however, the White House always wins. Washington society eventually accepted the Monroes' rules of etiquette, along with their hospitality. Moreover, future First Ladies would be forever indebted to Elizabeth Monroe for freeing them from the demands of local sociabilities.

The Monroes' successors, John Quincy Adams and his wife, continued the high style of entertaining, bringing to it a background of the longest and most varied diplomatic and social experience abroad that any President has ever had. John Quincy, son of the first President to live in the White House, had served in United States missions at many courts, including Prussia, the Netherlands, and England. His wife, Louisa

Admiring guests inspect the "exceedingly fine" presents sent to Nellie Grant on her marriage to Algernon Charles Frederick Sartoris in May 1874. Frank Leslie's Illustrated Newspaper lists a "dessert set of eighty-four silver pieces," a "very handsome silver ice-cream service," and a lace handkerchief "such as sell for $500."

FRANK LESLIE'S
ILLUSTRATED
NEWSPAPER

Entered according to Act of Congress, in the year 1886, by Mrs. FRANK LESLIE, in the Office of the Librarian of Congress at Washington.—Entered at the Post Office, New York, N.Y., as Second-class Matter.

No. 1,603.—Vol. LXII.]   NEW YORK—FOR THE WEEK ENDING JUNE 12, 1886.   [PRICE, 10 CENTS. $4.00 YEARLY. 13 WEEKS, $1.00.

WASHINGTON, D. C.— THE WEDDING AT THE WHITE HOUSE, JUNE 2ND— THE MOTHER'S KISS.

FROM A SKETCH BY C. BUNNELL.—SEE PAGE 261.

Johnson Adams, born in London to an American father and an English mother, was a brilliant scholar and an accomplished hostess. Well read in Greek, French, and English literature, she wrote verse in French, played the harp and spinet, and maintained her equanimity under the heavy pressure of official entertaining.

"This evening was the sixth drawing-room," President Adams wrote in his diary after one of the public levees that were held every fortnight. "Very much crowded; sixteen Senators, perhaps sixty members of the House of Representatives, and multitudes of strangers…these parties are becoming more and more insupportable…."

As a conscientious New Englander, however, Adams never shirked his duty. He met punctiliously with his guests and served even more elaborate refreshments than had his predecessor. The loaded trays carried by waiters threading their way through crowded state rooms held ice cream, coffee, tea, cakes, jellies, wines, and liqueurs—plus various imported West Indian fruits in season.

Perhaps the most notable dinner presided over by John Quincy Adams was one in 1825 honoring the Marquis de Lafayette on his 68th birthday. The French hero of the Revolutionary War, who was paying a return visit to America, responded thus to the President's toasts to his and George Washington's birthdays: "To the Fourth of July," he said, "the birthday of liberty in both continents."

The Adams family also held a historic wedding. On February 25, 1828, young John Adams, grandson of one President and son of another, married his cousin Mary Catherine Hellen, who had lived with the family in the White House. The event marks the only time that a President's son has been wed in the mansion. The ceremony was held in the first-floor oval room—now the Blue Room—which was decorated then in crimson and gold.

It was not an altogether happy occasion for the Adams family. The President had disapproved of the match, probably because fickle Mary Catherine had flirted earlier with John's two brothers. But the reception provided a bright note to an otherwise gloomy election year. Even the reserved and formal President unbent enough to dance the Virginia reel.

John Quincy Adams ended his one-term Presidency in deep chagrin over his defeat by the West's magnetic general, Andrew Jackson. He did not linger to attend the inaugural ceremonies, which culminated in the most boisterous celebration ever seen at the White House.

The enthusiastic followers of the veteran Indian fighter and hero of

Grover Cleveland, the only President married in the White House, accepts congratulations while his bride, Frances Folsom, kisses her mother. Rice and old slippers (above) rain down as the Clevelands leave on their honeymoon.

the Battle of New Orleans poured into Washington from far and near to see the "People's President" installed in the highest post of the land. Frontiersmen, clerks, and bankers, some with wives and children, jammed the boardinghouses and hotels, slept in the streets, and whooped it up in the bars. "It was like the inundation of the northern barbarians into Rome…," said one eyewitness.

After applauding Jackson's inaugural address at the Capitol, the crowd moved on to enjoy the White House reception—to the accompaniment of crashing china and glassware. Attendants lured many of the unruly guests out to the lawn for punch served from buckets.

Inside, merrymakers stood in muddy boots on satin chairs to catch a glimpse of their new leader, while would-be handshakers backed him against the wall. The President escaped the mob's further embrace only by slipping out and spending the night at the "Wigwam," as capital residents had nicknamed the nearby Gadsby's Hotel.

YET THE RUDE OPENING of the Jackson Administration was far from an accurate foretaste of "Old Hickory's" tenure in the White House. Accustomed to the fine surroundings of his Tennessee plantation, the President immediately sought appropriations from Congress to improve the mansion, which the legislators had allowed to fall into a shabby state during the Adams Administration.

Throughout Jackson's two terms, a willing Congress provided him with nearly $50,000 to refurbish the house and to build the massive, rectangular North Portico to complement the gracefully curving south entrance added by Monroe.

Before the end of Jackson's first year, the great East Room was at last completely and handsomely furnished to permit the ceremonial use for which it was originally planned. The President was particularly interested in having the Monroe chairs repaired and reupholstered, according to one account, so that people would not be kept "standing upon their legs as they do before kings and emperors."

At his official receptions and suppers, Jackson also offered guests sumptuous repasts, including the best wines and liqueurs, and every kind of meat and fowl the lush new land afforded.

But Jackson himself had little interest in either food or drink. Even his victory at the polls was an empty one, for he had come to the White House in deep grief—and cold fury. His beloved wife, Rachel, had died of a heart attack shortly after his election, and he believed her death was caused by malicious campaign gossip that stirred up an old scandal about their marriage. They had wed 30 years earlier in the mistaken belief that her first husband had obtained a divorce. After the divorce was granted, the Jacksons remarried, but political enemies never stopped blackening her name.

The President was thus disposed to defend the reputation of another woman he felt to be similarly maligned. A "petticoat war" erupted when wives of high government officials refused to receive pretty Peggy

O'Neale Eaton, daughter of an innkeeper and wife of Jackson's Secretary of War, John Eaton. Though Jackson pressured their husbands, the wives still would not recognize the woman they accused of accepting Eaton's attentions before her first husband died. All but one of Jackson's Cabinet Members resigned before the problem was resolved by the appointment of Eaton first as governor of Florida and then in 1836 as United States minister to Spain.

The last open house held by Jackson was almost as rowdy as his first. On the eve of leaving office in 1837, he was presented with a 1,400-pound cheese. Placing the huge gift in the north hall, he invited the public to come and eat as much as they liked in celebration of George Washington's birthday. The people came in droves. What they didn't eat dropped on the floor and was trod into the carpets; the smell lingered for weeks. The whole affair, some said, effectively discouraged public entertaining by incoming President Martin Van Buren, who was Jackson's Vice President and his handpicked choice for the nation's top office.

FRANK LESLIE'S ILLUSTRATED NEWSPAPER, FEBRUARY 21, 1885, TINTED BY P. HALL BAGLIE

Cartoon satirizes curious rural visitors to the White House after its 1882 redecoration by President Chester A. Arthur.

Whatever his reason, Van Buren—a widower for years—discontinued all public receptions except those on New Year's Day and July 4. Instead of the openhanded hospitality of the Jackson era, he arranged small, exclusive dinner parties, where both friendly and opposing political leaders traded lively repartee.

The President's four bachelor sons, who lived with him and shared his social and political interests, presented an irresistible challenge to Washington matchmakers. Dolley Madison, who was by now an aging but still romantic widow, won the prize by introducing Van Buren's eldest son, Abraham, to Angelica Singleton, a lovely young relative of hers then visiting the capital from South Carolina.

As Mrs. Abraham Van Buren, charming Angelica made a perfect hostess for her father-in-law. But the President's enemies found a rich lode of political capital in what they pictured as selfish high living in the Executive Mansion while the country suffered from a severe depression. Congressman Charles Ogle of Pennsylvania led the attack in blocking an appropriation of $3,665 for the mansion's maintenance.

In what would become famous as the "Gold Spoon Speech," he described Van Buren as one who used "knives, forks, and spoons of gold, that he may dine in the style of the monarchs of Europe." He spent "the People's cash in…green finger cups, in which to wash his pretty tapering, soft, white lily fingers," and ate fancy French foods instead of good

American "'hog and hominy,' 'fried meat and gravy'...with a mug of 'hard cider.'" Van Buren's defenders assembled figures to prove that their man actually was costing the taxpayers less for house expenses than had any other President. But the gold-spoon image had been created, and in 1840 the voters elected the President's opponent, William Henry Harrison, candidate of the Whig "Log Cabin and Hard Cider" Party.

The next shift in administrations came with a suddenness no one could have anticipated. Former General Harrison, hero of a famous Indian battle on the Tippecanoe River, was at 68 the oldest man to become President up to that time. He rode horseback to the Capitol and in an icy wind delivered the longest inaugural speech in history. Other exposures to wintry weather followed, leading to a cold that turned into pneumonia. One month after his inauguration, he was dead.

Harrison's wife, Anna, was the only First Lady who never acted in her official role. She did not even see the White House. At the time of the inauguration she was unable to stand the rough coach-and-steamer trip from her home on the Ohio frontier. She was about to leave when a messenger rode up with news of the President's death. It was too late to attend the state funeral for her husband—the first President to die in office. She remained in Ohio, where Harrison had made his career—and where their grandson, Benjamin Harrison, would start on his path to the Presidency nearly half a century later.

Thus the White House received an unexpected master in John Tyler, who as the Vice Presidential candidate had been the last half of Harrison's catchy campaign slogan, "Tippecanoe and Tyler Too."

PRESIDENT TYLER, labeled "His Accidency" by unkind critics, was destined to remain in the mansion only a single term. But he brought to it in turn two wives as different as they could be. Gentle Letitia, his first wife and mother of eight children, led the retiring life of an invalid until her death in 1842. Acting in her stead, her daughter-in-law, Priscilla (Mrs. Robert Tyler), performed as a highly successful official hostess on such glittering occasions as the state dinner and ball given for the Prince de Joinville, son of Louis Philippe of France.

Letitia Tyler appeared in company only once in the White House, at the wedding of her daughter Elizabeth to William Waller of Virginia. Wearing a simple gown and a soft lace cap that framed her handsome dark eyes, she sat quietly during the festivities.

"Lizzie has had quite a grand wedding," Mrs. Robert Tyler wrote of the event, which all Washington society attended. Dolley Madison, now 73 and popular as ever, was there, as well as the eloquent Daniel Webster, Tyler's Secretary of State and a great friend of the family.

In his deep, resonant voice, Webster quoted Sir Walter Scott when someone remarked that the President's pretty daughter was giving up capital "belleship" to live in quiet Williamsburg.

"Love rules the court, the camp, the grove...," he said—and spoke more prophetically than he knew. For in June 1844, eight months before

"Princess Alice," on the arm of her father, President Theodore Roosevelt, descends the grand stairway for her 1906 marriage to Congressman Nicholas Longworth. "It wasn't like that at all," Mrs. Longworth said in later years of the newspaper illustration. "We came down in the elevator in the back and walked down the hall to the East Room."

NEW YORK JOURNAL AND AMERICAN, FEBRUARY 18, 1906, LIBRARY OF CONGRESS, TINTED BY P. HALL BAGLIE the end of his term, the widower President took a second wife in a private ceremony in New York City.

The bride, lighthearted 24-year-old Julia Gardiner—a belle at home and abroad before her marriage—frankly enjoyed the attention she received as the nation's First Lady. Seated in a large armchair on a platform in the Blue Room, the erstwhile "Rose of Long Island" greeted guests with the air of a queen. In a white satin ball gown and gleaming headdress adorned with diamonds and ostrich feathers, she led the dancing in the East Room as gentlemen whirled their partners in the then-daring waltz. At one reception she introduced a bouncy Bohemian dance called the polka and started it toward wide popularity.

After an especially triumphant evening, Julia Tyler wrote her mother with girlish delight, "the British Minister, Pakenham, was there…and devoted to me. At least fifty members of Congress paid their respects to me, and all at one time."

To pleasure-loving members of the capital's higher echelons, the dancing steps of the second Mrs. Tyler gave way far too quickly to the dogged tread of all-work-and-no-play President Polk, and his handsome but straitlaced Sarah, a devout Presbyterian. New rules permitted no dancing, card playing, or similar diversions.

The proper Polks did their duty, offering the required number of formal dinners and grand receptions, but no food or beverages refreshed the great dry public gatherings, which were famous for sedateness and sobriety. A guest who ventured to compliment the First Lady on the "genteel assemblage" at one of these receptions met Sarah Polk's dignified reply: "Sir, I have never seen it otherwise."

The next three Presidents—Zachary Taylor, Millard Fillmore, and Franklin Pierce—had little chance to enliven the Washington social scene. The popular former general, "Old Rough and Ready" Taylor, died after only 16 months in office. During that time his delicate wife, Margaret, had relied on their married daughter, Betty Bliss, to do the honors at official functions.

Ailing Abigail Fillmore also was forced to delegate many of her hostess chores to her daughter, Mary Abigail. Yet, as the President's wife, she managed to put in an appearance and to greet guests at a surprising number of dinners and receptions in spite of delicate health and the pain that came from standing on a permanently injured ankle.

One of the gloomiest periods in White House entertaining prevailed during the Pierce Administration, which began soon after the Pierces had seen their last surviving child, Benjamin, killed in a railroad accident.

To the Emperor and people of Germany and to Prince Henry of Prussia! Offering a toast, Theodore Roosevelt turns toward his guest of honor. At his left stands Sir Julian Pauncefote, the British Ambassador. Protocol had fretted the President—"Will the Prince take Mrs. Roosevelt [to dinner] while I walk in solemn state by myself? How do we do it anyhow?" His solution: a reception with ladies, followed by a stag dinner served in the East Room. Flags and eagles of the two countries brighten the menu for the Kaiser's brother.

Naturally limited at first, White House social functions continued thereafter in a stiff and somber atmosphere, which extended even to Mrs. Pierce's large table bouquets of rigidly wired japonicas.

The return of what a reporter called "joy and gladness in the Executive Mansion" came, ironically enough, in the ominous pre-Civil War term of President James Buchanan. One cause for joy was Buchanan's beautiful young niece and ward, Harriet Lane. As his official hostess, she presided over so many brilliant balls and sumptuous banquets that the White House was compared to a European court; and it frequently drew titled travelers.

Journalists also wrote about the first diplomatic mission to Washington from Imperial Japan in the spring of 1860. Delivering a commercial treaty, the 60-member entourage created a sensation in the mansion's East Room, where curious Americans climbed on chairs to view the envoys' exotic clothing and hairstyles.

As a final social coup in his politically weak administration, President Buchanan welcomed the Prince of Wales, later Britain's Edward VII, as a houseguest. Miss Lane arranged a state dinner with royal protocol, followed by fireworks on the lawn. But the public reception for the prince turned into a roughhouse.

"The Royal party have certainly seen Democracy unshackled for once," wrote a New York correspondent. "The rush…was terrible. People clambered in and jumped out of the windows…."

DURING THE CIVIL WAR, White House entertaining took a new direction. The Union capital was crowded with Northern Army and Navy officers, war contractors, and assorted visitors who came to see President Lincoln and to share the First Family's hospitality. Special dinners and receptions were given for high government officials, staff officers, and diplomats.

To the President's weekly public levees came motley crowds of soldiers and day laborers along with the most fashionable ladies and gentlemen. Attired "with gloves and without gloves; clean and dirty…," they all pressed toward "the tall, rapidly bobbing head of the good 'Abe,' as he shook hands with his guests," recalled one bystander; and "when anyone he knew came along, he bent himself down to the necessary level, and seemed to whisper a few words in the ear, in pleasant, homely fashion."

Mary Lincoln held afternoon receptions, too, and carefully planned major social events. But nothing she did could please her relentless critics. If she served fine food, the First Lady was wasting money while brave boys died at the front. If she held only a reception instead of a formal dinner, her critics said she must be saving money for the personal finery that everyone knew to be her weakness. Yet the same carping public committed shocking acts of vandalism in the President's home.

Guests at Lincoln's second inaugural reception cut souvenirs of floral designs from brocaded window draperies and lace curtains; damage was extensive. After Lincoln's assassination, ruthless collectors ravaged the house. "Silver and dining ware were carried off…," wrote an eyewitness. "It was plundered not only of ornaments but of heavy articles of furniture. Costly sofas and chairs were cut and injured."

Following the Civil War, White House hospitality continued to reflect the attitudes of each new set of residents as they adapted themselves and their house to changing times. When Andrew Johnson and his family moved into the shabby building in the summer of 1865, they brought to its renovation a sturdy common sense that might well have served as an example to politicians during the turbulent days of Reconstruction.

"We are plain people from the mountains of Tennessee," said the Johnsons' older daughter, Martha Patterson, who directed most of the work and took over as official hostess for her invalid mother. "I trust too much will not be expected of us," she added, and then proceeded to extend the family's hospitality with natural good taste and a charm that surprised and won over many Washington sophisticates.

The Johnsons also showed how "plain people" could stand with dignity during the terrible weeks before the President's impeachment trial ended in his vindication. But it was a miserable time for all.

The inauguration of popular Union general Ulysses S. Grant on March 4, 1869, finally opened the floodgates for long-deferred capital celebrations. Mrs. Grant relished her role as mistress of the White House. She found it, she wrote, "a garden spot of orchids…a constant feast of cleverness and wit, with men who were the brainiest…and women unrivalled for beauty, talent and tact."

William Howard Taft receives socialites on the south lawn.

The Grants entertained often and lavishly. In 1874 King David Kalakaua of the Sandwich Islands—now Hawaii—became the first ruling monarch to visit the White House. At a state dinner in his honor, three of the King's retinue stood behind him, and one examined each dish before his master accepted it.

The peak of the Grants' social activity came when their idolized daughter, Ellen (Nellie), wed a young Englishman, Algernon Charles Frederick Sartoris, whom she had met on a trip abroad. The 18-year-old bride, dressed in white satin trimmed with yards of Brussels round-point lace, was married amid elaborate floral decorations in the great East Room. The wedding breakfast included an awesome assortment of elegant dishes for the most fashionable social event of the season. One participant at the feast was plainly unhappy, however. Tears filled the eyes of President Grant, who was losing his only daughter.

If the Grant Administration typified mid-Victorian style in heavy food and intricate decor, President and Mrs. Rutherford B. Hayes followed as perfect examples of the era's ideal of moral rectitude. Few White House scenes were ever more sedate than the Sunday-evening hymn sings and prayers that Congressional and Cabinet friends shared with the Presidential family. No alcoholic beverage was served at any function—a prohibition that later earned Mrs. Hayes the nickname of "Lemonade Lucy" and brought a quip from one guest that "water flowed like wine."

The more relaxed yet intellectual social atmosphere that marked the beginning of James A. Garfield's term as the next President is often obscured by the tragedy of his assassination. Both he and his wife, Lucretia, were warm, cultured people. A classical scholar, Garfield sometimes performed the trick of simultaneously writing Greek with one hand and Latin with the other. Mrs. Garfield was perhaps the first First Lady to initiate serious research on White House history.

Then, without warning, the bright six-month tenure of the Garfields ended on July 2, 1881, with shots fired by a demented office seeker. When the new Chief Executive, former Vice President Chester A. Arthur, took over, he began making some of the most drastic changes yet seen in the appearance of the mansion.

"I will not live in a house like this," he said after inspecting the accumulation of mixed and battered furniture and ornaments. Nor did he. Arthur sold at public auction 24 wagonloads of discards, lavishly redecorated the mansion, and installed the famous Tiffany glass screen on the formal first floor.

A rich widower, President Arthur became the most eligible catch in town. His huge wardrobe and swanky carriage were topics of conversation, his elegant dinners the most sought after. But he remained an elusive prospect and left as he came, a widower.

The people's next choice was America's second bachelor President, Grover Cleveland, who soon placed himself beyond the reach of contriving matchmakers by choosing his own bride.

T HE WEDDING of the only President to marry in the White House created a furor in 1886, when 49-year-old Cleveland took as his wife lovely 21-year-old Frances Folsom, daughter of his former law partner. The couple planned a private wedding; the bridegroom issued fewer than 40 handwritten invitations to close friends and relatives. But Cleveland had the mansion turned into a bower of flowers for the occasion, and church bells all over the city announced the end of the ceremony as a 21-gun salute boomed from the Navy Yard.

As a hostess, Frances Cleveland proved as capable as she was beautiful. She organized functions well in advance and showed her stamina by shaking hands with an estimated 9,000 guests at one public reception. She arranged at-home days so that all women who wished to meet her could. She held two receptions a week, one on Saturdays so that working women could attend.

Indeed, energetic Mrs. Cleveland so enjoyed life in the White House that she left tearfully in 1889, remarking to a member of the house staff that she and her husband would be back. Four years later

President and Mrs. Dwight D. Eisenhower greet Queen Elizabeth II and Prince Philip of Great Britain on their arrival at the North Portico. Of his royal guests' hectic, historic, and cordial four-day stay at the White House in October 1957, Eisenhower recalled, "This was one ceremonial visit that we were sorry to see end."

Grace and glitter in the glare of photographers' lights: With President and Mrs. John F. Kennedy, Shah Mohammad Reza Pahlavi of Iran and his Empress Farah enter the White House for a state dinner during their visit in April 1962. Below, the Kennedys and their guests applaud renowned cellist Pablo Casals after his East Room concert in 1961.

she kept her promise. Cleveland was reelected and became the only President to serve nonconsecutive terms.

The Victorian Age gave us two more First Ladies, each representative of the period in her own way. Caroline Scott Harrison, wife of Benjamin Harrison, brought to her new role the same energy she had shown in church and club work back in Ohio. A model of domesticity, she presided over the White House with genteel efficiency.

President William McKinley's wife, Ida, embodied a no less typically Victorian image of the delicate female. Though in poor health, she made valiant efforts to cope with official schedules. She attended exhausting state dinners, at which the usual seating arrangement was changed to place her beside her devoted husband, who could thus see to her needs. From a chair near the receiving line at receptions, Ida greeted guests but held a bouquet to foil handshakers.

As the 20th century arrived, it was no coincidence that the dynamic character and deeds of Theodore Roosevelt reflected America's exuberance, growing power, and influence. By moving his offices to the new West Wing and remodeling the mansion's state rooms after the simple elegance of the early federal period, the President at once gained quarters for increasing executive business and created a more appropriate setting for the nation's official entertaining. From December 1902, when the renovation was completed, social functions began to take on the more regulated character of modern times. The Roosevelts employed the first White House social secretary, and the President delegated a government official to untangle sticky problems of precedence involving diplomatic and political rivalries.

Roosevelt imparted his own ebullience to every White House event—from a reunion with the Rough Riders of the Spanish-American War to a Japanese jujitsu exhibition in the East Room, or to formal state functions, such as the reception and spectacular stag dinner he tendered Prince Henry of Prussia. T.R.'s charming wife, Edith, brought to her official duties a poise that led the President's military aide, Archie Butt, to write that she spent seven years as First Lady "without ever having made a mistake."

But it was Roosevelt's eldest daughter, Alice—by his first wife, who had died shortly after childbirth—who set off the social fireworks of the administration. "Princess Alice," as the newspapers called her, became the most headlined debutante and bride of her generation. A thousand guests came to the White House wedding and reception when she married Congressman Nicholas Longworth of Ohio. Her gifts included rare silks and jade sent by the Empress Dowager of China, a pearl necklace presented by the Cuban government, a feather duster, and a hogshead of popcorn.

Dancers of the Harkness House for Ballet Arts perform the premiere of "Classi- ▷ cal Symphony" at the dedication of a new portable stage, designed to match the decor of the East Room and given to the White House in September 1965.

Japanese guests in silk kimonos and obis chat with Mrs. Johnson in the State Dining Room. This 1965 reception followed ceremonies at the Tidal Basin, where the First Lady planted two flowering cherry trees—part of a gift of 3,800 saplings from Japan. Mrs. William Howard Taft planted the first cherry tree beside the Tidal Basin in 1912.

The last eight decades of social history at the White House have clearly shown how life in the Executive Residence has been colored by each family's personality and background.

President and Mrs. William H. Taft gave a touch of the Orient to their quarters by introducing furnishings from the Philippines, where he had served as the first American civil governor. The Tafts were also first to entertain on the terraced roof of the new west extension, where they sat at wicker tables under Chinese lanterns swaying in the breeze.

Woodrow Wilson, who like John Tyler became a widower while in office and who also brought a second wife to the mansion, had firm ideas of his role as host. Regardless of pressures, he refused to invite anyone to the White House to further even the most precious of his programs. "I will not permit my home to be used for political purposes," Wilson declared. And although he presided with good humor at official parties, he preferred small dinners in the Jeffersonian manner—animated by witty and intellectual conversation.

President Wilson and his first wife, Ellen, launched two of their daughters into marriage at the White House. The wedding of their second daughter, Jessie, to law professor Francis B. Sayre was the outstanding social event of the administration, though perhaps not so grandiose as one headline writer put it: "NATIONS OF ALL THE WORLD DO

British Prime Minister Harold Wilson, seated to the right of President Johnson, leans forward to hear Secretary of State Dean Rusk report on world affairs in 1965. British and American officials conferred on mutual problems at the working luncheon. The wallpaper in the President's Dining Room portrays a less friendly period between the two countries—the Revolutionary War.

HOMAGE TO WHITE HOUSE BRIDE AS SHE TAKES SOLEMN VOWS AMID SCENES OF UNEQUALED SPLENDOR."

In contrast, the marriage of the Wilsons' youngest daughter, Eleanor, to Secretary of the Treasury William Gibbs McAdoo six months later was held to a minimum of display because of the fast-failing health of her mother.

After the grim days of World War I, and the gloom of Wilson's long illness, brought on by the strain of his lost campaign for the League of Nations, the arrival of genial Warren G. Harding seemed to bring back the pleasant days of "normalcy" he had promised.

NOT ONLY DID THE NEW PRESIDENT and his wife, Florence, reopen the doors for large and frequent official gatherings, but they also dined almost daily with Harding's card-playing cronies and other close friends. They welcomed the public for tours of the mansion; on such occasions, Mrs. Harding sometimes appeared unexpectedly and shook hands with astonished, delighted sightseers. Though she suffered from a chronic kidney ailment, she energetically went about her duties as First Lady.

Then, suddenly, following the President's heart attack and death during a trip to the West in 1923, the convivial period ended. To the Executive

Mansion came the rock-ribbed New Englander and former Vice President, Calvin Coolidge, and his charming wife, Grace.

Social life during the Coolidge Administration was notable for the many anecdotes it produced concerning the granite reserve and wry humor of the President. The early-morning breakfasts to which Coolidge invited Members of Congress—often to the dismay of late sleepers—gave capital raconteurs some of their best stories. One told of the time the President poured coffee and cream into his saucer. As a few guests followed suit, Coolidge calmly put the saucer on the floor for his dog.

The most famous guest of the time, loquacious Queen Marie of Romania, was entertained at a state dinner in 1926. According to Chief Usher Ike Hoover, the queen made strenuous efforts to get "Silent Cal" to talk, but "was not any more successful than others who had tried it before." The whole affair was odd, the chief usher noted, for the visit, including ceremonial greetings, the meal, and farewells, took only an hour and 45 minutes.

Yet, in the matter of etiquette, President Coolidge inaugurated what has become an indispensable aid in conducting state visits. Following an awkward incident in which wartime enemies were seated together at an official dinner, he established a Protocol Office in the State Department to handle procedures for such visits. Today its chief has a staff of more than 70 people to arrange programs, determine precedence, and suggest food preferences to fit the specific needs of each delegation.

White House entertaining reached new heights when President Herbert Hoover assumed office amid a seemingly endless boom economy. Even after the stock market crashed in the autumn of 1929, the wealthy President and his wife, Lou, continued to invite a record number of guests for breakfast, lunch, and dinner, though they personally met the expenses not only for their private parties but also for many of the official ones.

No one could assume, however, that such hospitality marked indifference to the nation's problems. The Quaker President had long shown his humanity in war and postwar relief work in food distribution, and no President ever worked harder than Hoover as he labored to solve the country's gargantuan economic troubles. At times he would gulp his meals so fast, a member of the domestic staff recalled, that "the servants made bets on how long it would take…'Nine minutes, fifteen seconds,' or whatever…."

FRANKLIN DELANO ROOSEVELT and his big, gregarious clan came next, to meet the challenge of the Depression and usher in the longest, most varied social period yet. Eleanor Roosevelt in her book *This I Remember* listed a staggering number of official and personal luncheons, teas, dinners, receptions, and other programs.

In one year alone, President and Mrs. Roosevelt put up 323 houseguests, served meals to 4,729 people, and offered refreshments at teas and receptions to 14,056 others. The assorted guests pouring into and

Following their wedding in the East Room in 1967, Lynda Johnson Robb and Charles Robb (below) walk under swords held by six of the bridegroom's Marine comrades. On the arm of her father, Tricia Nixon (above) enters the Rose Garden in 1971 for the first outdoor wedding in White House history. After the ceremony, Mr. and Mrs. Edward Finch Cox return to the mansion for a reception.

out of the mansion between March 1933 and April 1945 included students, poets, playwrights, labor leaders, nuclear scientists, prime ministers, and presidents. British Prime Minister Winston Churchill came often, and the mysterious visitor of 1942, known only as Mr. Brown, turned out to be Soviet Foreign Minister V. M. Molotov on a mission to speed up the opening of an Allied second front in Europe.

World War II gave a regal dimension to the Roosevelts' hospitality with the appearance of royal refugees fleeing Nazi occupation in Europe. Some, such as the Crown Prince and Princess of Norway and Queen Wilhelmina of the Netherlands, became temporary houseguests. Others, such as the Kings of Greece and Yugoslavia, were briefly feted. Older Washingtonians recall the White House visit of Britain's King George VI and Queen Elizabeth just before war erupted in 1939. Down the hall from the family rooms on the second floor, the King occupied the Lincoln suite, his Queen, the Rose suite, later called the Queens' Bedroom. Screens separated the royal and presidential quarters.

Thus each administration has left its social imprint here since John and Abigail Adams first welcomed leaders of official Washington to their formal "levees."

By the time of President Harry S. Truman and his wife, Bess, the "season" had expanded to include half a dozen state dinners and as many Congressional and other large receptions. Some were so well attended that guests stood almost shoulder to shoulder.

At a reception in 1948, the chandelier in the Blue Room tinkled a warning that the structure was in critically shaky condition. During the following four years, while the White House underwent reconstruction, the Trumans lived across the street in the government's guest residence, Blair House. In 1951 Britain's Princess Elizabeth and her husband, Philip, Duke of Edinburgh, spent several days there with the Trumans.

The next year, the presidential family moved back into the restored Executive Mansion just in time to welcome as houseguests Queen Juliana of the Netherlands and her consort, Prince Bernhard.

But capital life was changing in the postwar era. State visitors came so frequently from newly independent nations and as a result of foreign-policy conferences and fast modern transport that the White House could no longer accommodate them.

Since the latter part of the Eisenhower Administration, most official guests have stayed at Blair House during their state visits. In fact, only once during Eisenhower's second term did such guests sleep in the mansion. Elizabeth II, Queen of Great Britain, and Prince Philip

President Ford stands to toast Queen Elizabeth II of Great Britain at a Bicentennial dinner in her honor on July 7, 1976. Lilies and greenery decorate the pavilion erected in the Rose Garden for the occasion. After dinner (above), Mrs. Ford dances with Prince Philip in the State Dining Room.

occupied the Rose and Lincoln suites, as had her mother and father nearly 20 years before.

Under the lively direction of John F. and Jacqueline Kennedy in the early 1960s, official entertaining changed further. President Kennedy banished receiving lines whenever possible and chatted informally with guests in the connecting state rooms. Shorter, simpler dinners allowed the guests more time to dance and to watch performances of internationally known musicians, ballet dancers, opera singers, jazz stars, and Shakespearean actors.

Then came the crack of rifle shots in Dallas—and a black interlude of international mourning for the bright, lost promise of a murdered President. When social life returned to the White House, the new host brought

Trees ablaze with tiny lights offer a glittery backdrop for the barbecue given by President and Mrs. Jimmy Carter on the west terrace during the visit of the Japanese prime minister in May 1979. Like the Tafts, who were the first to hold dinners on the rooftop terrace, the Carters frequently entertained outdoors. In June 1978 a jazz festival on the south lawn featured Eubie Blake, pounding out ragtime with a gusto that denied his 95 years (below).

with him a quarter century of capital friendships and service, first as Representative and Senator from Texas, then as Vice President. It was not surprising that an atmosphere of Texas Americana pervaded the private and official parties of Lyndon B. Johnson and his wife, Claudia, better known by her childhood nickname, "Lady Bird."

Informal cordiality also warmed two of the most publicized social events ever held in Washington—the weddings of the Johnson daughters, Luci and Lynda. The news coverage demonstrated the public's avid interest in every detail of a First Family's life. Scores of reporters, photographers, and television crews recorded Luci's August 1966 church wedding to Patrick J. Nugent, of Illinois, and the reception at the flower-adorned mansion. When Lynda married Capt. Charles S. Robb of the

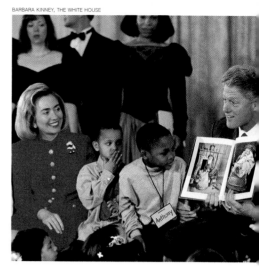

U.S. Marine Corps, 16 months later, both ceremony and reception took place in the White House. Telephones, typewriters, and closed-circuit television were provided for some attending members of the news media.

In January 1969 the spotlight on executive entertaining moved from the Johnsons to the Nixons, another family with two daughters. But the resemblance ended there, for President and Mrs. Nixon, like those who went before, soon produced an entertainment pattern all their own that included programs ranging from rock concerts to comedy routines to Shakespearean drama. One innovation was a series of Sunday-morning services attended by associates and friends of the family. Held in the East Room and presided over by leaders of various faiths, the services were followed by a social hour and refreshments in the State Dining Room.

But nothing attracts more attention than a wedding. The Nixons' younger daughter, Julie, missed most of the fanfare by marrying David Eisenhower, grandson of the former President, in New York City, shortly before her father was inaugurated.

Her sister, Tricia, however, chose the White House for her marriage to law student Edward Finch Cox of New York. She arranged for the ceremony to be performed in the famous Rose Garden. Thus, on June 12, 1971, she became the first President's daughter to have an outdoor wedding at the Executive Mansion.

Some 400 guests were seated in the garden, which resembled an old-fashioned valentine decorated with masses of roses, lilies, and petunias. Standing before the altar, in an open, wrought-iron pavilion laced with white blossoms, the President gave the bride away. Afterward, blond, diminutive Tricia, wearing a lacy Juliet cap, cascading veil, and white organdy dress, walked back to the mansion with her tall, smiling bridegroom to open the reception and dancing that followed.

Tricia's wedding marked the social high point of her family's tenure. As events unfolded over the next three years, the Nixon Administration ended in political scandals and the President's resignation—and a new family in the old house.

From August 1974 to January 1977 the Gerald Fords made their own

Barbara Bush and Betty Ford (opposite, far left) applaud the Boys Choir of Harlem, which was appearing before present and former Senate wives after a luncheon in June 1989. In December 1994, President Clinton entertains a group of Washington, D.C., schoolchildren gathered in the State Dining Room with a reading of "The Night Before Christmas." Hillary Rodham Clinton and guests in the Diplomatic Reception Room (left) enjoy a March 1995 performance by several students from New York's Ramapo High School.

brand of White House history. Among happier events on the social side guests may remember lively musical and theatrical programs capped by dancing in the big Entrance Hall. There Betty Ford, who once studied modern dance with the noted Martha Graham Dance Company of New York, whirled gracefully with the President and other partners.

With the Georgia Carters, still another regional design went into the tapestry of White House hospitality, which never ceases to repeat the infinite variety of American life.

"Natural," "spontaneous," and "family oriented" were often used by the media to describe the Carters' southern style. Yet, if some found elements of close-knit, small-town entertaining at Jimmy and Rosalynn Carter's receptions and dinners, there was no doubt that the top-notch American and European performers they introduced on the East Room stage rivaled the world-famous musicians, ballet dancers, and opera stars who enchanted audiences during the Kennedy Administration.

Still, the more it changes, the more hospitality retains its symbolic meaning in the house that belongs to all Americans. And this is never more so than when a President and his wife receive visiting dignitaries representing a cross section of global power and influence.

Where else could you find dinner guests who included 18 heads of Latin American states, 25 U.S. Senators, a former President, Gerald Ford, and a former First Lady, Lady Bird Johnson? This spectacular event occurred during the Carter Administration in September 1977, after the ceremonial signing of the treaties to transfer the Panama Canal to the Republic of Panama.

Behind the glitter and ceremony of such state affairs, elaborate planning goes into making sure each is tailored to fit the national culture and individual tastes of the guests of honor. To assure the success of the meal, the Reagans even tried out the complete dinner, down to the last detail, a week or ten days before the event.

Guest lists to state dinners serve to promote goodwill or enhance diplomatic dialogue. For instance, when Emperor Akihito and Empress Michiko of Japan came to the White House, the Clintons invited the heads of many major American firms, who in the past had felt shut out of Japanese markets. The formal state dinner for South African President Nelson Mandela included leading African Americans, such as actress Alfre Woodard, poet Maya Angelou, and journalists Carl Rowan and Dorothy Gilliam.

At smaller soirees for 40 to 60 guests, those invited represent a mix of old friends and prominent figures in politics, business, and the arts. Mrs. Clinton enjoys this kind of socializing, noting, "We have a wonderful opportunity to bring people together across a lot of lines that they would not cross otherwise." They have developed their own style of entertaining, which Mrs. Clinton describes as "both respectful of traditions, but also perhaps a little more fun and informal."

Decorations and table settings for formal White House dinners, following tradition, are classic and elegant. Frequently in use is the set of china that Nancy Reagan acquired—red rimmed with a gold band—as well as the Johnson plates, which feature Lady Bird Johnson's favorite motif, flowers. Centerpieces of roses, atop tables gracefully draped with gold damask or floral tablecloths, complement the china.

The White House chef, Walter Scheib, and his staff favor a generally

Following the tradition accorded state visitors, President Clinton and his newly arrived guest, Emperor Akihito of Japan, review the troops on the south lawn in June 1994. The ceremony included a 21-gun salute and the Fife and Drum Corps playing a lively "Yankee Doodle." For the state dinner that evening, the first of the Clinton Administration, the President and Mrs. Clinton received the Emperor and Empress Michiko at the North Portico, then escorted them upstairs for a brief informal conversation and a view of the south lawn from the Truman Balcony. Then they descended the Grand Staircase and received the other guests before heading out to the Rose Garden for dinner. On this visit to the White House, the royal couple promoted friendship and goodwill between Japan and the United States.

BOB MCNEELY, THE WHITE HOUSE

lean American cuisine. Hillary Clinton has worked with them to make the menus "a little more nutritious and lower in fat, but still maintaining the beauty of the service and the presentation of the food." Turbot, shrimp, and crab are frequently served, as are quail and pheasant, cooked in light herb sauces and served with fresh vegetables. For Chancellor Helmut Kohl's state dinner, Scheib prepared pan-seared salmon with key lime and ginger, pheasant breast with wild mushroom risotto and tomato basil coulis.

Petit fours were once commonly served to White House guests for dessert, but they have been replaced over the years by healthier, lighter fare. At the dinner for King Hassan II of Morocco, dessert consisted of apricot sherbet and frozen date mousse.

An elegant blending of American style and international taste comes to the fore in the musical entertainment at the White House. King Hassan enjoyed an after-dinner concert by the renowned Modern Jazz Quartet. The Japanese Emperor, who plays the cello himself, was royally entertained by the superb cellist Mstislav Rostropovich. At smaller, informal events, the Clintons often have the Marine Band and the Army's Strolling Strings playing show tunes after dinner.

3

THE FIRST FAMILY
AT HOME

DESPITE ALL OF THE COMFORTS and privileges that come to a President and his family, homemaking in a house that is also a national monument has several drawbacks.

When President Coolidge arrived at the White House in 1923, he tried to continue his pleasant after-dinner habit of sitting on his front porch— the great North Portico—and watching the people go by on Pennsylvania Avenue. So many pedestrians stopped to stare at him, however, that he gave up this modest form of relaxation.

President Coolidge once invited a Missouri Senator friend to accompany him on an evening walk outside the White House grounds. As they returned to the mansion, the Senator remarked facetiously, "I wonder who lives there."

"Nobody," replied the President. "They just come and go."

Coolidge's wry remark was only half true. Though Chief Executives have moved in and out with regularity, the White House has always been a place of extremely personal living. Indeed, the attention commanded by the Presidency intensifies and exaggerates the normal joys and sorrows of everyday family experience, the high moments of birth and death that are part of life here as in any other home.

Accentuated problems, too, face each First Lady in her highly visible role as the President's wife and as the mistress of a semipublic

In a quiet moment, Frances Cleveland catches up on her correspondence in the family quarters. Through the years, First Families have attempted, with varying success, to lead normal personal lives in the hectic White House.

"Here we gather every evening," remarked President Hayes of his library, today's Yellow Oval Room. Family and friends listen while Carl Schurz, Secretary of the Interior, coaxes "fantasias and caprices" from the keys. On Sunday nights, Cabinet officers and Senators joined in singing hymns— "There is a land of pure delight," and "A few more years shall roll."

building. The public is keenly interested in, and often feels free to criticize, the way she runs her house, selects her dresses, or chooses to style her hair. Mrs. Hoover told of receiving a letter from an indignant tourist who complained about a mended curtain she had seen in one of the rooms. Eleanor Roosevelt remarked that she sometimes felt she was no longer clothing herself "but dressing a public monument."

The clothes and hairdos of a President's wife may sway fashions everywhere. Jacqueline Kennedy's fitted dresses, cloth coats, and bouffant hairstyle were copied around the world. When designers drastically lengthened skirts in 1970, many reporters asked Mrs. Nixon just how far from the floor she would wear her hems. About this time, French President Georges Pompidou, accompanied by his wife, arrived for a state visit—and Mrs. Pompidou's midi skirts received almost as much press coverage as did her husband's politics.

Betty Ford, who made her living as a model when she was a young woman studying dance, stayed in step with—and sometimes ahead of—current vogues. Some of Rosalynn Carter's outfits came from top American designers; but she showed her taste for simple dress by bringing her own sewing machine with her to the White House.

Nancy Reagan, who had a slim, model-like figure, preferred classic daytime suits and elegant evening gowns. During the ceremony at the Smithsonian Institution celebrating the donation of her first inaugural ball gown to the National Museum of American History, she remarked, "I feel like Cinderella." Barbara Bush, in turn, donated her inaugural gown to the First Ladies exhibition—a sapphire-blue dress with a square-necked velvet bodice and a full satin skirt.

In 1994 Hillary Clinton donated her lacy, violet inaugural gown, noting, "It is a bittersweet moment to give this dress up." Mrs. Clinton's taste in daytime clothes tends toward stylish suits complemented by either a scarf or jewelry. For formal White House events, she prefers floor-length evening dresses by American designers.

AS HUSBAND AND FATHER, nearly every President has known the frustration, especially in periods of national stress, of trying to find enough time to be with his family. When Garfield's son Harry was 17 and fell in love with the daughter of one of his father's best friends, a month passed before young Garfield was able to get the President alone to talk about it.

Eleanor Roosevelt wrote in her memoirs that at times the Roosevelt boys had to make appointments to see their father. On one occasion, she recalled, FDR was so deep in an important document that he seemed unconscious of one son's account of a personal matter, and the young man left without getting his father's opinion. "I doubt if the public realizes," Mrs. Roosevelt commented, "the price that the whole family pays in curtailment of opportunity to live a close family life."

One of the most endearing aspects of life in the Executive Mansion can be glimpsed from the hundreds of stories that have come down

CLINEDINST PHOTOGRAPH, LIBRARY OF CONGRESS (BELOW); COURTESY MARTHENA HARRISON WILLIAMS

Models of decorum here, grandchildren of Benjamin Harrison enjoy a party in the second-floor nursery of the White House. Marthena Harrison reaches tentatively into a bowl, Mary McKee tastes a cookie, and Benjamin (Baby) McKee watches from his rocker. Presiding: the President's daughter, Mrs. James Robert McKee (left), and his daughter-in-law, Mrs. Russell B. Harrison. At right, President Wilson cradles his first granddaughter, Ellen Wilson McAdoo, in 1915.

through the years about the many children who have lived, and sometimes grown up, in the big white house where something new and exciting is always happening.

The very young ones were usually grandchildren, since few men have reached the top rung of the political ladder in their early years. And the first of all the children whose shouts and laughter echoed through the mansion's broad corridors was the four-year-old granddaughter of John and Abigail Adams.

Little Susanna arrived in November 1800 in the carriage bringing her grandmother, who was belatedly joining President Adams in the dank, unfinished building. The little girl distressed her grandparents soon afterward by developing whooping cough, but she recovered, and lived to tell her own small granddaughter Susanna of her adventures in the White House.

Jefferson's eight years in the Presidency were cheered and brightened by the visits of his married daughters, Martha Randolph and Maria Eppes. On one of these visits, in the winter of 1805, Mrs. Randolph gave birth to her eighth child—named James Madison Randolph—the first baby born in the Executive Mansion.

Jefferson was a devoted father and a fond grandfather, always ready for a race on the lawn or a romp inside with his daughters' bright youngsters. In her chronicles of early Washington life, Margaret Bayard Smith recalled his remark to her when she mentioned the amusement that children afforded adults. "Yes," Jefferson said, "it is only with them that a grave man can play the fool."

T HOUGH ANDREW AND RACHEL JACKSON never had children of their own, the widowed President surrounded himself with Rachel's visiting nieces and nephews and their offspring. Three of the six or more youngsters usually on hand were born in the White House. These three were children of Rachel's nephew Andrew Jackson Donelson, who stayed with the President as his private secretary, and his lovely wife, Emily, who served as Jackson's official hostess.

"Uncle Andrew," as the children called the President, often attended personally to the needs and wants of his adopted family; he rolled their baby carriages through the halls, comforted them in teething, and frequently joined in their games.

Golden-haired Mary Emily Donelson wrote long afterward about a happy Christmas season that she spent with the President, and of a party that Jackson gave for the youngsters, their playmates, and other Washington children. Though the world knew him as a man of "iron will and fierce, ungovernable temper...," she said, "he was the gentlest, tenderest, most patient of men at his own fireside."

"Mrs. Adams is winding silk from several hundred silkworms that she has ▷ been rearing," President John Quincy Adams recorded in his diary on June 23, 1828. Hot water dissolves the gum that cements the cocoons' filaments.

The most photographed presidential grandchild of the 19th century must have been "Baby McKee," who lived in the White House with grandfather Benjamin Harrison and his four-generation family during the early 1890s. Among the numerous family members, which included parents, grandparents, aunt, uncle, cousins, and great-grandfather, mischievous little Benjamin gained a reputation with the press as the President's favorite who could do no wrong.

Professional and amateur photographers were just then discovering George Eastman's new, easy-to-operate Kodak box camera—one of the first to use roll film—and they haunted the grounds, hoping to get pictures of little Benjamin. Soon, published photographs showed the active and appealing youngster as he played with his dog, led the Marine Band, or drove his own goat cart about the grounds.

The goat, called "His Whiskers" by the coachman, once ran away with Baby McKee, giving reporters one of their best stories about him. As His Whiskers darted off with the boy and raced down the White House driveway onto Pennsylvania Avenue, the portly President himself, dressed in top hat and frock coat, followed in hot pursuit.

With such a start in the 1890s, illustrated news coverage of the younger members of the Chief Executive's family has never slackened.

Roosevelt grandchildren, 13 in all, gather with Eleanor and FDR on his fourth inaugural, January 20, 1945. Their grandmother Eleanor had slides, sandboxes, and swings built for the younger children on the south lawn.

STORIES AND PICTURES of Franklin Roosevelt's grandchildren Anna Eleanor and Curtis Dall made their nicknames, "Sistie" and "Buzzie," household words throughout the country during their stay in the White House. In January 1945, near the end of Roosevelt's 12-year administration, all 13 of his grandchildren attended his historic fourth inauguration—the largest group of grandchildren ever assembled at the Executive Mansion.

In their time, President and Mrs. Eisenhower delighted in the visits of their four grandchildren, David, Barbara Anne, Susan, and Mary Jean. Though none of these children of John and Barbara Eisenhower actually lived in the White House, the youngest, Mary Jean, was christened in the Blue Room, and all found plenty of toys and playground equipment on hand for their amusement.

The children called their grandmother "Mimi," and a revealing story shows how they regarded Grandfather Eisenhower. Someone had asked small David his name. "Dwight David Eisenhower," he replied.

"Then who's that?" probed the questioner, pointing to the President.

"That's Ike," said the boy.

It may surprise many who recall pictures of Abraham Lincoln's lined and aging face that he and his wife, 52 and 43 respectively, were among the younger presidential couples, and that they were the first to bring to the White House a child of their own who was under 10. Thomas, or "Tad," was 7, William 10, and their brother Robert, who would be off at college most of the time, 17, when Lincoln and his family arrived in Washington from Illinois to become part of the nation's most tragic era.

Abraham and Mary Lincoln were loving and indulgent parents who often said, "Let the children have a good time." This the children did, and the President's friends and colleagues quite probably felt at times that he was too permissive when he failed to punish Tad for bombarding the door with his toy cannon during a Cabinet meeting, or when the boy stopped his father's callers to sell refreshments and wheedle money for war charities at stands he set up at the mansion.

But the President found Tad's pranks a welcome relief from sorrow and responsibility; and both Lincoln and his wife took pride in Tad's generous nature, as well as in the talent that gentle, cheerful Willie revealed in the verses and short speeches he composed.

Lincoln thoroughly enjoyed, too, the physical activity of a good wrestling match with his boys, and he encouraged them in the fun of collecting and raising pets of various kinds, including dogs, ponies, and goats. Lincoln bought Tad a pair of goats at $5 each. He got his money's worth in amusement when the youngster hitched the animals to a kitchen chair and drove his unlikely rig through the East Room, to the consternation of a group of visiting ladies from Boston. When one of the goats disappeared, he wrote a whimsical letter saying that "poor Nanny" had last been seen "chewing her little cud, on the middle of Tad's bed...."

A devastating blow came to the family when Willie developed a severe fever and died soon afterward, on February 20, 1862. The President shouldered his grief with his other burdens, but high-strung, erratic Mary Lincoln was inconsolable. She turned to spiritualism in the hope of receiving a message from beyond the grave, and arranged at least one session with a popular medium of the day at the Soldiers' Home—the Lincolns' "summer White House."

For a while Mrs. Lincoln believed her lost boy had returned. "He comes to me every night," she told her sister, "and stands at the foot of my bed, with the same sweet, adorable smile...." Later she wrote, "...the loved & idolized being, comes no more."

Some insisted that Lincoln himself attended one of the spiritualist meetings, though it was never made clear whether this was to please his wife, to satisfy his own curiosity, born of a streak of mysticism, or to show up the medium's tricks. One story had the President joking about conflicting suggestions offered him by "Napoleon," "Lafayette," and other spirits on the conduct of the war. "Their talk and advice," he reportedly said, "sound very much like the talk of my Cabinet."

On the eve of Union victory early in April 1865, Lincoln described a strange dream to his wife and a good friend. In the dream, he said, he was awakened from a deep sleep by a "pitiful sobbing." Getting up, he followed the wailing sound to the East Room, and there he found a catafalque surrounded by mourners. On it he saw a still figure shrouded in funeral garb, the face covered. "The President," one of the soldiers standing in the honor guard whispered to Lincoln, "...killed by an assassin."

HANK WALKER, LIFE MAGAZINE © TIME, INC.

Within two weeks, Abraham Lincoln had been shot by John Wilkes Booth in Ford's Theatre. In the East Room, Lincoln's body lay on a catafalque, surrounded by mourners as foretold by the dream.

In a room above, Mary Lincoln lay prostrated by grief. While Tad and Robert sought to comfort her, they could hear the sound of weeping from long lines of people passing the bier to pay their last respects.

President and Mrs. Grant, the next couple to arrive at the Executive Mansion with young children of their own, were fortunate in leading one of the happiest and most normal of family lives in the history of the White House. The Grants' affectionate and outgoing children—three sons

Storybook romance between David Eisenhower and Julie Nixon captured the country's imagination. The couple met as shy 8-year-olds at Ike's second inaugural (above). On December 22, 1968, they were married in New York.

80

and a daughter named Nellie—ranged in age from 11 to 18. The middle son, Ulysses Simpson Jr., was called "Buck" because he was born in the Buckeye State of Ohio. Both he and his older brother, Frederick, worked for the President as confidential secretaries during Grant's second term.

Fred, a graduate of West Point, married Ida Maria Honoré in October 1874, though the wedding was not held at the White House as Nellie's had been. Later the couple came to live in the mansion, and here a daughter was born and named Julia, after her grandmother.

One of the liveliest and warmest accounts of the Grants comes from the fun-loving youngest son, Jesse. In his book of reminiscences, *In the Days of My Father, General Grant,* he told of his joy in the gift of a small but powerful telescope, which he used to study the heavens. He recalled the gatherings of neighborhood friends who "flocked to the White House…the largest and best playground available." The "lot was our playground, in good weather," he wrote, "…the big, airy basement…was reserved for rain or storm."

WHITE HOUSE PHOTOGRAPH

Jesse also became an ardent stamp collector. In his impatience to receive an order that he had paid for with $5 out of his savings, he appealed to his father, suggesting that the dealer be prodded by a letter from the Secretary of State, the Secretary of War, or Kelly, a policeman on White House duty. The matter was solemnly debated at a Cabinet meeting with Jesse pleading his case. It was finally decided to have Kelly write the following: "I am a Capitol Policeman. I can arrest anybody, anywhere, at any time, for anything. I want you to send those stamps to Jesse Grant right at once."

The stamps came.

Wrote Jesse in memory of his family: "The love of my parents for each other and their devotion to us children made no impression on me then. I had never known anything different. Appreciation and understanding come to me now, filling me with content."

As had Grant, both Rutherford B. Hayes and James A. Garfield brought to the Executive Mansion in turn a warmhearted, close-knit family. Each included four boys and a girl. Moreover, the two families were old friends, linked by common Ohio origins and congressional service in Washington.

Fanny Hayes and Mollie Garfield, both 14, sat together at Garfield's inauguration, behind the mother of the President-elect—the first mother to see her son take the oath of office. Mollie continued her friendship with Fanny after the family, including Grandmother Garfield, moved into

Julie and David Eisenhower often visited the White House during her father's Presidency. They now live near Philadelphia. She has written a book about her mother, and David has completed a biographical volume about his grandfather.

the mansion. When Mollie gave a luncheon for ten young girls, she remembered her obligations as a hostess in the White House, and seated Fanny, as the daughter of a past President, on her right.

With Garfield's accession to the Presidency, his two older sons, Harry and James, stayed at the White House, studying there under a private tutor instead of completing the remaining months of their prep-school terms. Thus they, too, happened to be with the rest of the family, along with Mollie and the two younger boys, Irvin and Abram, during most of the last six months of their father's life.

For the rest of their lives, Harry and James Garfield would look back in horror upon the morning of July 2, 1881, when they and the President were planning to join Mrs. Garfield, who was then vacationing in Long Branch, New Jersey.

The two boys were in high spirits at the prospect of the trip, and President Garfield, a large and active man despite his bookish bent, joined them in a bit of horseplay before they all departed for the Washington depot of the Baltimore and Potomac Railway. Less than an hour later, an office-seeking fanatic, Charles Guiteau, fired two shots at Garfield as he entered the waiting room. Garfield fell; physicians rushed to the scene, and a horse-drawn police ambulance soon returned the gravely wounded President to the White House.

For more than two months, Garfield battled for life in his second-floor bedroom at the mansion, while his wife and children waited and prayed. Outside the gates, frequent bulletins kept the public informed of the condition of the man in the sickroom. A metal-detecting device developed by Alexander Graham Bell was used in an attempt to locate the bullet, but the effort failed because of interference from the bed's steel springs.

In the hope that sea air might help cure the President, he was transferred by train—with every precaution taken to prevent jolting—to the ocean resort of Elberon at Long Branch, New Jersey.

But no air could combat the infection that had developed. Garfield died on September 19, and his body was carried directly to the Capitol to lie in state in the Rotunda. It was the only time in history that a President who had died in office did not lie in state in the East Room.

T HE ONLY PRESIDENT'S CHILD born in the mansion was Esther Cleveland, the second daughter of Grover and Frances Cleveland. Esther's sister Ruth, who had arrived during the interlude between Cleveland's two terms, was almost two years old at the time of Esther's birth in 1893. Before the President's second term ended, another little girl, Marion, was born at the Clevelands' summer home in Massachusetts.

"The Cleveland children were…much beloved by everyone around the place," wrote durable Chief Usher Ike Hoover, who would serve in ten administrations. "We often wished that more of them had been born in the White House…."

Staid rooms resound to boyish laughter as presidential children turn the White House into an arena for a boisterous game. The Garfield boys—Irvin, 11, and Abram, 9—maneuver cumbersome velocipedes during an East Room pillow fight. At left, Tad and Willie Lincoln improvise a quieter game—a costume drama in the White House attic. In this painting, Willie wears some of his mother's cast-off clothes, Tad the uniform and trappings of a Union brigadier general.

PAINTINGS BY ALEX ROSS, 1962

The public seemed to feel much the same way about the three pretty little girls. Gifts and advice on how to rear them poured into the White House from all over the country.

One Washington boy organized what he called an honor guard for Ruth. Marching his young company up to the door, he asked for, and received, an interview with the President. Cleveland regretted he was too busy to review the troops, but he delegated the role to Mrs. Cleveland, who complied with pleasure.

Tad Lincoln, given a courtesy commission by Secretary of War Edwin M. Stanton, wears a colonel's uniform. His White House days ended after a black-draped drum (opposite) sounded at his father's funeral; many citizens hung mourning ribbons in their windows.

Another, less pleasant, incident occurred when a group of curious visitors gathered around Ruth and her nurse during an outing on the grounds. One of the women picked up the child and passed her around to the accompaniment of pats and kisses. The episode so alarmed Mrs. Cleveland that from then on the gates to the south lawn were closed to the public—an exclusion that resulted in cruel and baseless rumors that the child was deformed.

Four and a half years after the departure of the demure little Cleveland girls, the uninhibited children of Theodore Roosevelt came on with the force of a hurricane. "A nervous person had no business around the White House in those days," observed Ike Hoover in describing their behavior. "Places that had not seen a human being for years were now made alive with the howls and laughter of these newcomers….Nothing was too sacred for their amusement and no place too good for a playroom."

Among other pranks, the five younger children—aged 3 to 14 when the Roosevelts arrived—slid down the stairways on trays stolen from the pantry, stalked the halls on stilts, and bicycled and skated on newly polished floors. Speeding in his toy wagon, Quentin, the youngest, rammed the full-length portrait of Mrs. Rutherford B. Hayes, leaving a hole.

Their lovely, self-willed half sister, Alice, then 17, contributed to the uproar in her own way. She refused to go away to boarding school, but she later made trips around the country, as well as to Cuba, Puerto Rico, and Asia. From shipboard in the Pacific came the story that "Princess Alice" had jumped, fully dressed, into the ship's pool.

"I can do one of two things," the President once said. "I can be President of the United States, or I can control Alice."

The Roosevelt children also kept a small zoo of pets. Underfoot, inside and out, were a badger, a bear, raccoons, rabbits, turtles, parrots, pigs, cats, dogs, rats, guinea pigs, snakes, and a calico pony named Algonquin. When Archie had the measles, his brothers entertained him by leading the pony into his second-floor bedroom, after riding up in the President's elevator.

When Quentin grew old enough, he was sent to a nearby public school, and he often brought his pals home to add to the commotion. One of these friends, Earle Looker, many years later wrote a book called *The White House Gang*. In it he described the hilarious adventures of the boys and the quick and just punishment meted out by the President after such antics as the spattering of Andrew Jackson's portrait with spitballs.

T.R., as the gang called him—not disrespectfully but with a mixture of affection and awe—had an amazing knowledge of the interests and needs of active children. When official business was slow, he sometimes joined the youngsters for games in the White House attic.

On one such occasion, as the President was about to catch up with a boy he was chasing, young Earle turned out the light. A crash followed, and when Earle found the switch again, he saw Roosevelt holding his head and leaning against a post, from which a nail protruded shockingly close to the height of his eyes.

"I'm quite all right," he told the contrite boys, "but never, n-e-v-e-r, never again, turn off a light when anybody is near a post!"

Mrs. Roosevelt managed to preside with grace and calm over her large, boisterous group of children, and T.R. once summed up his feelings in a letter to their son Kermit: "I don't think that any family has ever enjoyed the White House more than we have."

TEN MORE ADMINISTRATIONS would follow that of Grover Cleveland before the cry of a President's infant was again heard inside the Executive Mansion. Then, early in 1961, came John and Jacqueline Kennedy with their two-month-old baby, John Jr., and his engaging sister, Caroline, three years old.

Soon newspaper and magazine editors were publishing stories and pictures of the youngsters' third-floor playroom where the Eisenhower grandchildren had romped not long before; of the new tree house, swings, and other playground equipment behind south-lawn shrubbery; of Caroline's pet canary Robin, her pony Macaroni, and her dog Pushinka, the gift of Soviet Premier Nikita Khrushchev.

Multiplying anecdotes told how "John-John" had refused to greet the Grand Duchess of Luxembourg because he had not been given his usual cookie and ginger ale; how Caroline had presented India's Prime Minister Jawaharlal Nehru with a rose for his buttonhole; and what she said when reporters asked what her father was doing. "Oh, he's upstairs with his shoes and socks off," she said, "not doing anything."

As a child of the Space Age, Caroline Kennedy made news again when she asked John Glenn not about his pioneering flight around the earth but about another orbital test with chimpanzees. "Where's the monkey?" she asked the astronaut.

By restricting photographs and limiting access to her children, Mrs. Kennedy sought to protect them from the effects of so much concentrated attention. She established a kindergarten at home, as had Mrs. Cleveland, so that Caroline and little John could play with children of their own age, away from the public eye.

Lack of personal privacy is an old complaint of Presidents and

Florence Harding with Laddie Boy.

Baby McKee holds the reins of His Whiskers, a goat presented to him by grand-

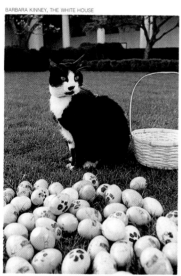

The Clintons' cat, Socks, at Easter.

Mrs. Bush and Ranger keep watch.

Mrs. Coolidge, raccoon Rebecca.

Him and Her, the Johnson beagles.

President Wilson's sheep crop White House lawns during World War I.

father Benjamin Harrison.   *FDR's dog, Fala, begs a handout.*   *Amy Carter and Misty Malarky Ying Yang.*

Caroline Kennedy rides Macaroni across the south grounds.   *Nancy Reagan's dog, Rex.*

Theodore Roosevelt, Jr., macaw Eli.   *White House policeman holds Algonquin's reins for Quentin Roosevelt.*

their wives. Certainly no couple suffered more from it than did the Clevelands on their honeymoon in 1886, when the "ghouls of the press," as Cleveland later called them, followed the newlyweds to a lodge at a Maryland mountain resort. Equipped with spyglasses and cameras, the newsmen went to incredible lengths to get stories and pictures.

During the election campaign of 1888, scurrilous rumors of Cleveland's mistreatment of his young wife gained such wide circulation that Mrs. Cleveland issued an indignant denial.

"I can wish the women of our Country no greater blessing," she said, "than that their homes and lives may be as happy, and their husbands may be as kind, attentive, considerate and affectionate as mine."

Today, reporters are not permitted to get as close to the First Family as they sometimes did in the past. Nor can individual members of the public enter the White House grounds without an official pass or previous clearance by authorities. Armed, highly trained men of the Executive Protective Service, a uniformed branch of the Secret Service, are stationed in gatehouses along the high iron fence and closely check the identity of all callers. The Secret Service maintains various other security measures in carrying out its responsibility of guarding the President—a responsibility given to it in 1901, after McKinley's assassination. Specific regulations followed; one of the most important requires Secret Service agents to remain near the Chief Executive at all times. The objective is to

Caroline Kennedy and her infant brother, John Jr., arrive at the White House for the first time on February 4, 1961. The portrait at left has been published as one of Mrs. Cleveland and baby Marion, later Mrs. John Harlan Amen; Mrs. Amen, however, believed the portrait to show her sister Esther, born in the White House in 1893.

offer maximum safeguards with a minimum of interference, but many Presidents have grown restive under the attention.

While Taft conceded that the record of assassinations was such that "Congress would be quite derelict" in disregarding it, he added that it was difficult for a Chief Executive "to avoid the feeling…that he was under surveillance rather than under protection."

Theodore Roosevelt wrote to a friend: "The secret service men are a very small but very necessary thorn in the flesh." Then he went on to express his belief that no effort could prevent an assault upon his life and quoted Lincoln's remark that "though it would be safer for a President to live in a cage, it would interfere with his business."

Since a 1917 law extended Secret Service protection to other family members, unmarried sons and daughters of Presidents have faced the choice of giving up dates or accepting the company—however discreet— of an agent of the Service.

John Coolidge's classmates at Amherst joked that John would have to "elope from his agent" if he wanted to marry anyone. And Margaret Truman in her book *Souvenir* gives an account of the "handicap the Secret Service offers to escorts and beaus."

She had made up her mind, she wrote, not to marry while she lived in the White House. But she asked the reader "to consider the effect of saying good night to a boy at the door…in a blaze of floodlights, with

Susan Ford focuses on her father in the Oval Office as he reviews some of her work. Coached by White House staff photographer David Hume Kennerly, Susan began taking pictures for a photography class at Holton-Arms School. For her senior project, she submitted a portfolio of behind-the-scenes glimpses of life in the White House.

With deep concern, but inadequate medical resources, physicians wait with Mrs. Garfield as the President struggles to recover from a wound inflicted by an assassin on July 2, 1881. A crowd gathers outside the White House (top, left) awaiting the medical bulletin issued each morning; a mounted courier departs to inform the Cabinet of the President's condition, and a little girl brings a bouquet for the wounded Chief Executive. Above, Alexander Graham Bell, hoping to locate the bullet, listens with the telephone-like receiver of an electrical device he invented for detecting metal; steel springs in the mattress interfered. All efforts to save the President failed, and he died on September 19, 1881.

a Secret Service man in attendance. There is not much you can do except shake hands, and that's no way to get engaged."

Subsequent legislation now requires the Secret Service to guard not only the President and his family but also the President-elect, the Vice President, their families, as well as former Presidents, their widows and minor children, presidential candidates, and top officials from abroad. The cost is great, but in these days of political terrorism and random violence, arguments for cutbacks have been easily overruled.

On March 30, 1981, another attempt to assassinate an American President again underscored Roosevelt's point that no amount of precautions can eliminate such attacks. Unnoticed by the crowd standing outside a leading hotel in the nation's capital that day, a young man waited, handgun at the ready. When President Reagan emerged after a luncheon speech inside, a hail of bullets struck him, his press secretary, a Secret Service agent, and a Washington, D.C., policeman.

The President, at first unaware that he had been hit, was rushed to George Washington University Hospital. There, amid preparations for emergency surgery, he sought to relieve tensions by a spontaneous act of wit and courage that charmed the nation. "Honey, I forgot to duck," he told his wife on her arrival at the hospital. To the surgeons readying him for the operation, he quipped that he hoped they were Republicans. After more than three hours of surgery to remove the bullet, he cracked, "If I got this much attention in Hollywood, I'd never have left."

As the world knows now, the President made a remarkable recovery from his wound. The assailant—a 25-year-old drifter from Denver, Colorado, named John W. Hinckley, Jr.—was tried for the crime, and on June 22, 1982, was declared "not guilty by reason of insanity." He is now confined to a mental institution.

Today, the well-trained men and women of the Secret Service are never far from the Clinton family.

D ESPITE WHATEVER HAZARDS and lack of privacy our modern Presidents may endure, nothing could approach the shocking conditions that prevailed in family living arrangements until the beginning of the 20th century. The executive offices and family apartment shared space in the mansion itself. For much of the time, these rooms occupied opposite ends of the same floor.

In those days, a multitude of callers, ranging from tradesmen and patronage seekers to Cabinet officers and foreign dignitaries, streamed into and out of the north entrance. Some lounged as they waited in rooms on the state floor; others trudged up the public stairway to see the President or members of his staff. To avoid the often rough crowds, some of the older and more delicate wives of Presidents seldom ventured out of their west-side family quarters.

One of these was the first Mrs. Tyler. An invalid from a stroke suffered before she came to the White House, Letitia Tyler managed to run the household from her bedroom. This she did so efficiently and "so

A grieving figure, the stricken nation personified, appears atop William McKinley's mourning ribbon. Anarchist Leon Czolgosz approached the President and shot him as he stood in a receiving line at the Pan American Exposition at Buffalo, New York, on September 6, 1901.

quietly," wrote her admiring daughter-in-law, Priscilla, "that you can't tell when she does it."

Mrs. Zachary Taylor was another White House homebody. She received visitors only in her own quarters and limited her guests almost entirely to close friends and to relatives from the South.

Mrs. Taylor was a reluctant First Lady. The General, she felt, deserved a rest after 40 years of active duty that included service in the War of 1812, in skirmishes with frontier Indians, and in the Mexican War. During the election year of 1848, Taylor told supporters that his wife prayed nightly for his defeat. If he was unlucky enough to win the office, she had declared, it would shorten his life.

Mrs. Taylor's dark prophecy came true just months after her husband's inauguration. On July 4, 1850, the President sat for hours under the hot sun at a celebration on the grounds of the unfinished Washington Monument. Overheated and exhausted, he became ill of what was then called cholera morbus—the result, legend would say, of his having consumed too much iced milk and raw cherries.

Five days later, Zachary Taylor was dead. His grieving widow, secluded in her apartment, could hear the sounds of his office staff making way for the next occupants, and she could feel the vibrations of hammering as workmen assembled a catafalque in the East Room.

She could not bear to attend the ceremony, but she was forced to listen to its accompaniment, a sympathetic eyewitness reported, "as one band after another blared the funeral music…and the heavy guns boomed…to announce the final parting."

In later administrations, as executive responsibilities grew heavier and the number of visitors increased, presidential families faced ever greater inconveniences. A member of President Garfield's staff recalled in his memoirs that a mere acquaintance of the family "pushed himself in past the doors that marked the private domain…and took his afternoon siesta upon the most comfortable sofa he could find."

President Benjamin Harrison's wife, in an 1889 interview, complained that she was "being made a circus of…I've been a show, the whole family's been a show since Mr. Harrison was elected," she said. "All last fall I sat in my sewing room and watched the procession of feet pass across the parlour floor wearing their path into the nap, and disappear like the trail of a caravan into the General's room beyond. Day by day, I watched the path grow wider and deeper….But I don't propose to be made a circus of forever! If there's any privacy to be found in the White House, I propose to find it…."

Mrs. Harrison's solution to the problem called for Congress to adopt one of three drastic measures, for which she presented detailed architectural plans. The simplest of these would have provided the President with a separate residence and remodeled the mansion for entertaining and executive business only. The second design proposed the addition of wings to be used for office and guest suites. The most elaborate of the suggestions was to extend the house into a fantastic four-sided palace

Mourning badge—a miniature photograph trimmed in black velvet—depicts President Warren G. Harding. He died in San Francisco on August 2, 1923, after suffering a heart attack.

enclosing a huge court and fountains. Though Congress rejected Mrs. Harrison's projects, it did appropriate $35,000 for essential housecleaning and repairs to the deteriorating old house. Moreover, airing the need for reasonable family privacy and adequate office space helped pave the way for the future construction of wings on the west and east sides of the mansion.

F ROM THE BEGINNING, each President and his family have created a highly individual home within the Executive Mansion by furnishing and embellishing it in their own taste. Dolley Madison expressed her warm and vibrant personality in decorating the presidential quarters with bright yellow draperies and upholstery.

Sedate and proper Lucy Hayes had her bedroom walls "tinted pale blue, with panels of light gray and pink," as described by a woman correspondent permitted the rare privilege of seeing the Hayeses' private apartment in the 1870s.

Abigail Fillmore, a onetime schoolteacher, had met her husband-to-be when they attended school together. She obtained congressional funds for the first official library in the Executive Mansion. With a dictionary, histories, sets of Dickens, Thackeray, and other works, she filled the bookshelves installed in the upstairs sitting room. There, she and President Fillmore spent many quiet evenings reading and chatting, while their young daughter, Mary Abigail, played the piano or harp.

Equally revealing possessions have moved in and out of the White House with each successive family. With the Tafts, for instance, came the President's many lawbooks, recalling his long and distinguished legal career capped eventually by his appointment as Chief Justice of the United States.

The erudite Hoovers brought many mementos from their world travels: South American rugs, Asian art, caged songbirds—and books in various languages, including their own translation from Latin of an important 16th-century volume on mining. All helped Lou Hoover transform the broad, bare hall on the second floor into an inviting reception area for guests.

To the White House from Hyde Park, New York, Franklin and Eleanor Roosevelt shipped a wheelchair to carry the President along the family corridor. They also brought sturdy handcrafted furniture that had been scratched during family pillow fights and wrestling matches in which "Pa," with his powerful shoulders, won as often as his sons.

During the Trumans' time, the second floor held three pianos—appropriate symbols of the harmony that characterized the spunky, close-knit family from Independence, Missouri. One piano stood in the oval room that was then the President's study; their daughter, Margaret, practiced on another in her sitting room, where she also kept her record collection; while a third—a spinet in the hall—was frequently used for duets. The Truman family often spent evenings together, reading, playing, or listening to music.

Majestic columns of the South Portico frame Mrs. Dwight D. Eisenhower on the balcony as she waves a birthday greeting to her husband, 70 years old on October 14, 1960. After some 30 moves in 36 years of Army travels, the Eisenhowers lived longer together in the White House than anyplace else.

A few years later, when friends of President Eisenhower visited him in the upstairs oval room, which he, too, used as a study, they found displayed there a fascinating array of military and civilian awards, decorations, swords, and other gifts presented by world leaders. In his book *The White House Years*, the President wrote that he received visitors in the study "informally in the evening, whenever a somewhat homier atmosphere than could be obtained in my office was desirable." His "personal mementos of a fairly long life," he added, "…were kept there for a temporary period only, and later were transferred to a suitable museum—the Smithsonian, the Library of Congress, or the museum which bears my name in Abilene, Kansas."

After the Eisenhowers and the President's prized souvenirs went their separate ways, the changing scenes on the family floor continued

to mirror, in colors and furnishings, tastes and activities of each new group of White House occupants. Mrs. Eisenhower's feminine and frilly decor, with its "Mamie pink" accents in flowered slipcovers and draperies, gave way to Mrs. Kennedy's light-blue curtains and blue-and-white furnishings that showed to advantage against plain off-white walls in the private bedroom and sitting-room areas. American period pieces, French antiques, and valuable art objects began to appear in various places: the sitting halls that share the wide corridor; the Queens' and Lincoln Bedrooms, where visiting royalty had slept; and what was called the Treaty Room, then decorated in Victorian style. They gave visible evidence of Jacqueline Kennedy's program to restore to the White House furnishings that awaken a feeling of the historic past.

The Yellow Oval Room on the second floor has had the same color and Louis XVI furnishings, and has served the same function, for the last seven administrations. Mrs. Kennedy turned this room into a formal drawing room, and it has proved to be the most suitable place in the house to entertain state guests before dinners or luncheons given in their honor.

With the arrival of the Johnson family, Mrs. Johnson put her own signature on the look and use of the second-floor apartments. In her mainly green-and-yellow bedroom (symbolic, perhaps, of her project for the greening and beautification of Washington and the country) she set up a cozy working space, in which she dictated letters and speeches, and planned and directed her many activities.

"My house," John Kennedy, Jr., called the President's massive desk. He liked to hide behind its secret door while his father worked. Above, President Lincoln leafs through a photograph album with his youngest son, Tad.

Down the hall—in rooms that had lately known the toys of the Kennedy children—the Johnsons' teenage girls, Luci and Lynda, had their bedrooms until marriage took them both to homes of their own. And when President Nixon brought his family to the White House in 1969, his daughter Tricia moved into the suite that had been used by Lynda and Luci.

The following year, Tricia took television viewers on the first public showing of many of the rooms in the family living quarters. The tour started on the balcony overlooking the south lawn, with its lovely view of the Washington Monument and the Jefferson Memorial. Included were glimpses of the family dining and sitting rooms, and of the guest room called the Queens' Bedroom because five queens have slept there during state visits.

Tricia pointed out her mother's sitting room, in which she read and answered her mail, and the piano her father liked to play. She also described an incident in which Nixon built the flames so high in the fireplace of his private study adjoining the Lincoln Bedroom that an alarm sent White House firefighters rushing to the scene. There, they found him placidly writing a speech before the open fire, which, Tricia explained, was one of his great pleasures. In fact, she added, the President liked a cozy fire so much that he would light one even in warm weather and turn on the air conditioning.

After the Carters moved in, ten-year-old Amy occupied the bedroom that had been Caroline Kennedy's, then Luci Johnson's, then Tricia Nixon's. The youngest of the Carter offspring, Amy was by far the best known. Her tree house in the gnarled old cedar on the south lawn, her delight in reading, her violin lessons, pets, and school friends became part of the continuing White House small-fry chronicles that began with Susanna, granddaughter of John and Abigail Adams.

PRESIDENT AND MRS. REAGAN put their stamp on the second-floor family quarters, as well as on the expanded living space that was added to the third floor in 1927, during the Coolidge Administration. Most of this floor was then divided into bedroom, bath, and sitting-room apartments, which are available today for family members and personal guests. The remaining area served as space for storage and housekeeping. Mrs. Reagan's work on these floors complemented the refurbishing project begun by Mrs. Kennedy in 1961.

Mrs. Reagan sought private donations for her projects, and they eventually totalled more than $800,000. The money came from all over the country and ranged from a child's one-dollar contribution to ten thousand dollars or more from wealthy donors. The donations were largely spent on basic renovation, and for the conservation of certain valuable—and sometimes historically priceless—articles that had been in storage.

"Retrieving them was an exciting treasure hunt," said Mrs. Reagan of the scores of large and small objects that she and her decorator rediscovered and put back in use. Some of the most striking changes were

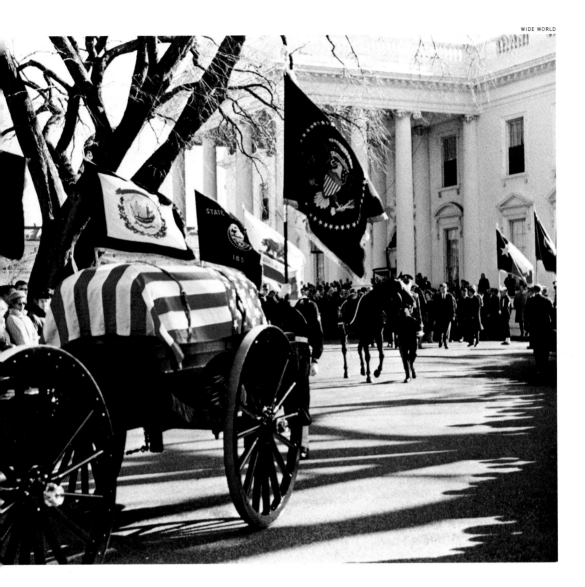

made on the third floor. Its wide central hall offers space in which to display refurbished, reupholstered, and regilded 19th-century federal furniture, as well as Currier & Ives prints, decorative objects, and sculpture. Of special interest to historians and antique buffs was a lacquered table in use in the sitting room at the east end of this floor. The table was brought as a gift to President Buchanan in 1860 by the first diplomatic mission sent from Imperial Japan to the United States.

Commanding the scene from the Center Hall of the second floor stands a gleaming mahogany desk, surrounded by pieces of furniture from the 18th and early 19th centuries. This octagonal pedestal writing desk, called a partners' desk, was made in England during the late 18th century. It can be separated into two parts, or combined—as in its present use—to make a central divider.

The Reagan redecoration focused chiefly on the second and third floors. But one elegant wanderer purchased by Monroe in 1817—a French Empire sofa—was returned to the Blue Room on the state floor. Sold at auction just before the Civil War, this gilded sofa, curved to fit the

Rolling caisson, followed by the President's flag, a riderless horse, and an assemblage of world leaders, bears John F. Kennedy from the White House to St. Matthew's Cathedral on November 25, 1963. An assassin had felled the President three days before in Dallas.

Like any other happily married couple, President and Mrs. Reagan enjoy sharing a quiet evening at home. When in the White House, they often ate dinner while watching the news in the President's second-floor study. This room contained furniture from their California home and a number of mementos, including the desk lamp made from a fire chief's silver horn.

room, came home in 1978, only to be stored again. Finally reclaimed and re-covered with blue silk, it joined seven of the original matching chairs.

For all its splendor, the White House is still the temporary family home of the man the people have elected to be their leader. The Clintons, like other presidential families, have brought many of their own belongings to make their quarters warm and welcoming. Among their treasured possessions are furniture, books, family photos, paintings, and personal memorabilia.

President Clinton, like George Bush before him, chose as his private office in the mansion a room where many Presidents in the late 19th century convened their Cabinet meetings. After Mrs. Hoover decorated it with reproductions of French furniture owned by President Monroe, this room was called the Monroe Room. In 1962 it was redecorated to resemble the Cabinet Room at the time of Ulysses S. Grant and was then renamed the Treaty Room, in commemoration of the many historic documents signed here.

The Clintons had the office redecorated, changing its light green walls to a faux-leather burgundy wallpaper, and replacing the floral chintz draperies with a bold red-, blue-, and-gold linen print. President Clinton uses as his desk the walnut conference table that has witnessed the signing of several historic documents, including the treaty marking the end of the Spanish-American War in 1898. Jimmy Carter had this table placed on the north grounds for the signing of the treaty between Egypt and Israel in March 1979. Then in September 1993, President Clinton had it moved to the south lawn for the signing of the peace accord between the Israelis and the PLO, and again on July 25, 1994, for the declaration ending the state of war between Jordan and Israel.

The magnificent Victorian table had been ordered in 1869, along with a set of "walnut French overstuffed chairs" by President Grant for his Cabinet Room. It is fitted with eight locking drawers—enough at the time for the President and each member of his Cabinet.

To accommodate the vast number of books that President Clinton brought with him to the White House, inlaid walnut bookcases have been installed here. Family photos and memorabilia, such as a collection of model cars, add a personal touch to this space, which is used by the President after hours.

Having delved into books about the White House in some depth, President and Mrs. Clinton want to preserve its traditions and history as much as possible. Mrs. Clinton asserts that her husband has acquired a deep historical sense about the place and the objects in it, remarking, "He gives a great tour and never gets tired of it."

Among those rooms the Clintons have redecorated is the Lincoln Sitting Room, off the Lincoln Bedroom, which is where family friends often spend the night. It has been redone in high Victorian style to complement the bedroom.

"People we've entertained have been so excited to see what could be called a historically correct room," Mrs. Clinton noted.

The walls have been painted a cream color, and ornate red-and-gold silk draperies hung. Artwork is from the Lincoln-Grant period, including a portrait of Grant over the fireplace and an 1864 print of Lincoln's New Year's reception at the White House.

Some of the rooms in the First Family's private quarters on the second and third floors have been redone in rose, peach, and green pastels. The West Sitting Hall, used as a living room, has a new yellow-and-blue carpet and newly upholstered furniture in yellow fabrics.

Here, as elsewhere in their family quarters, Mrs. Clinton explains, "We wanted to create an atmosphere that was warm and welcoming and suited to how a particular family lives and spends its time."

P RESIDENT AND MRS. CLINTON have one daughter, Chelsea, who was born in 1980. Mrs. Clinton is determined that her teenager "have as normal a life as possible" while the family lives in the White House. Chelsea's friends are in and out all the time, often coming over to swim in the pool, to try a few rounds at the bowling alley, or to join the Clintons in the special White House movie theater. When she's not doing schoolwork or having fun with her friends, Chelsea enjoys studying ballet, as well as going for walks and bike rides with her mother.

Every President's family takes its place in the flow of historic continuity, finding its own uses for the many nooks and crannies, public and

Rosalynn Carter greets sightseers on a morning tour of the White House.

Lady Bird Johnson plants a t

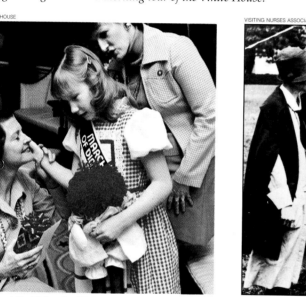

Betty Ford greets a blind March of Dimes Poster Child.

Grace Coolidge cuts a cake honoring the Visiting

In the White House Library, Barbara Bush reads to an attentive young audience.

Nancy Reagan presides ove

SHARON FARMER, THE WHITE HOUSE

Encourage your special someone to get a mammogram today! The risk of breast cancer increases as we get older.

Remember, regular mammograms save lives

on the north grounds.

In May 1995 Hillary Clinton speaks on the importance of getting annual mammograms.

First Ladies, in addition to their ceremonial duties as official hostess of the White House, increasingly pursue interests of their own. Eleanor Roosevelt championed the underprivileged and minority groups. Lady Bird Johnson initiated a national beautification program, which is renewed each year by blossoming trees and flower gardens. Betty Ford backed the Equal Rights Amendment. Rosalynn Carter addressed problems of the mentally ill, the elderly, and inner-city dwellers. Nancy Reagan joined the battle against drug abuse, particularly among young people. Barbara Bush focused her efforts on community-based causes, encouraging reading programs, feeding the homeless, and volunteering in a home for the aged. Hillary Rodham Clinton has served as informal advisor to her husband and has led the effort for health care reform. Building on her longtime interests, she has written and spoken out on issues involving children, education, and women's health and basic rights. She has widened the role of art at the White House, installing sculpture exhibits in the Jacqueline Kennedy Garden and using the Executive Mansion as a showcase for American crafts.

Nurses Association.

a conference on drug abuse.

Britain's Queen Elizabeth, wife of George VI, rides with Eleanor Roosevelt.

KEYSTONE PRESS AGENCY, JUNE 8, 1939

private spaces, within the various levels of the White House. Before Theodore Roosevelt separated his office from his home, the basement of the mansion—now called the Ground Floor—served as a workmen's area, cluttered with buckets and lumber, and defaced with pipes run through the walls. Today, this wide corridor shows off 19th-century American furnishings and displays on its walls a gallery of First Ladies' portraits. Off the corridor are several handsome rooms, including the Library, with its 19th-century portraits of Indian chiefs, and the Map Room, where FDR kept up with World War II's progress. The Clintons use these rooms frequently for private meetings and interviews.

BEHIND SUCH SCENES AND EVENTS, the men and women who have lived in the Executive Mansion have known the same happiness and frustration, pride, and misery that come to all of us. Every night, the gruff and lonely warrior, Andrew Jackson, performed a tender ritual. After removing the treasured miniature of his dead wife, Rachel, which he carried next to his heart, he would place it on the bedside table near her worn and faded Bible, so that he might see her face first on awakening in the morning.

In another of the family rooms, frail Eliza Johnson, devoted wife of Andrew for 41 years, rocked and sewed as she awaited word of the Senate vote at her husband's impeachment trial. "I knew he'd be acquitted," she said firmly, but with tears in her eyes, to the official who brought the good news. "I knew it."

Fashionable President Arthur, who lived luxuriously in the mansion during his one term in the 1880s, showed another side of his nature when he was alone. Like Jackson, he too was a recent widower and, like the earlier President, Arthur carried on a ritual of remembrance by ordering fresh roses to be placed daily next to the photograph of his lovely Ellen, which was displayed on a little easel in the transverse hall. He had been stunned by her sudden death from pneumonia in January 1880, at the age of 42, which left him alone with two children. He demonstrated his love and concern for their young daughter Nellie and their college-age son Alan by keeping them with him as much as possible.

One of the most touching scenes in the history of the great changeovers that have come to this house occurred in Eleanor Roosevelt's study on the second floor, after the death of her husband. Vice President Truman, summoned to the White House, arrived without knowing of the massive stroke that had ended the President's life at Warm Springs, Georgia. He heard the news from Mrs. Roosevelt.

As Truman described the meeting in his memoirs, he asked Mrs. Roosevelt, "Is there anything I can do for you?"

He would never forget her reply, he wrote. "Is there anything we can do for *you?*" she said. "For you are the one in trouble now."

Grief, both national and personal, has been too frequent a caller at the President's House. Eight Chief Executives have died in office, four of them by assassination.

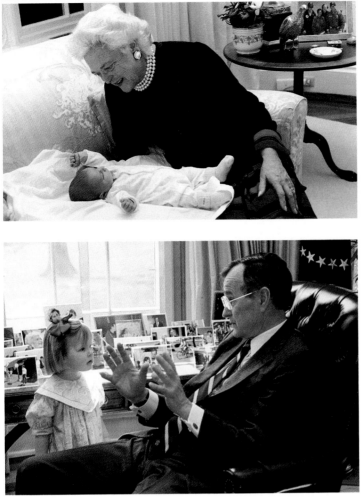

Barbara Bush beams at Margaret and Marvin Bush's son, Charles Walker. Walker's sister Marshall listens carefully as her grandfather explains something interesting. Even in the Oval Office, President Bush usually found time for a grandchild. All of his children and grandchildren visited the White House during his four years there.

Unlike the murders of Lincoln and Garfield, the third slaying was committed far from Washington. In September 1901 McKinley was shaking hands with visitors at the Pan American Exposition in Buffalo, New York, when a young man extended his left hand to the President, then shot him with a concealed revolver. The attack, by an anarchist named Leon Czolgosz, mortally wounded the President. McKinley died eight days later. The courage and strength in adversity of his widow, Ida, would amaze all who had known her as an almost helpless invalid.

Sixty-two years later, another assassin pressed a trigger in Dallas. As waves of shock spread from that Texas city, President John F. Kennedy lay dead in the prime of life. Then, once more, the casket of a Chief Executive rested in the black-draped East Room of the White House. From all over the globe came an extraordinary procession of the world's great—heads of state, prime ministers, and royalty—to pay their last respects and to share the grief of Kennedy's family and friends.

Yet whatever fate befalls the President, the Presidency never dies. Perhaps that is why Americans never tire of stories about the men who have held this office. And why millions turned on their television sets to follow the White House tours conducted by President Truman after the

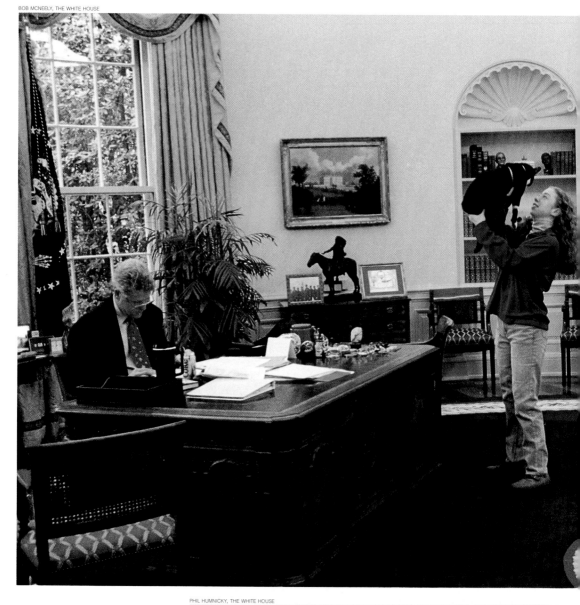

On Christmas Eve 1994, Chelsea Clinton and Socks visit the President in the Oval Office. Later, she and her father made a last-minute shopping trip to Georgetown. The First Family (right) stroll the south grounds before flying to Europe for the G7 Summit in July 1994. President Clinton and Chelsea (opposite) share an embrace in April 1995.

building's reconstruction, by Jacqueline Kennedy when she showed off antiques and artwork acquired through her special historical project, and by Tricia Nixon when she took her audience through family rooms on the second floor in 1970.

In September 1989, President and Mrs. Bush gave television viewers another personal tour of their family quarters. Then, in 1995, the Clintons treated millions of viewers to a look at the freshly refurbished Blue and East Rooms.

ONE OF THE MOST UNUSUAL TOURS was led by Mrs. Eisenhower in 1959. Her guests were all children or descendants of former Presidents, beginning with John Adams. Eight were sons and daughters of Chief Executives from Cleveland to Eisenhower. History traveled with the party as past residents of the house moved upstairs and down, swapping anecdotes about how it was when they knew "life with father" here.

Alice Roosevelt Longworth recalled the three circular Victorian ottomans, crowned by potted palms, that once stood in the East Room: "...the tops in the center came off," she said, "and my brothers and sister would hide there."

Helen Taft Manning, daughter of President Taft, remembered that her mother found the huge Lincoln bed too depressing a symbol for sleep; she relegated it to the attic.

Eleanor Wilson McAdoo wanted to quash the myth that pictured her father as "an intellectual snob" and "a grim old Presbyterian." In fact, she said, he was "our most amusing and gay companion."

A note of sadness crept into the nostalgia when the group came to the Lincoln Bedroom, which had been the room that John Coolidge shared with his younger brother, Calvin. Calvin, Jr., then barely 16, died in the summer of 1924—the result of blood poisoning that had developed after he rubbed a blister on his toe while playing tennis on the south grounds. "When he went," his father wrote in his autobiography, "the power and glory of the Presidency went with him."

All of the home-comers agreed that Mrs. Eisenhower's choice of colors had brightened the often somber family apartment. And all but one received a surprise when the group made its way down the center hall to the President's Office, at that time called the Monroe Room. It contained copies of President Monroe's furniture, including a replica of the desk on which he signed his famous Doctrine.

Pausing before this desk, Laurence Gouverneur Hoes, Monroe's great-great-grandson, pressed a panel that opened to reveal a secret compartment even Mrs. Eisenhower had not known about. Such a compartment, it turned out, had been discovered in the original desk in 1906, and young Hoes had been indirectly responsible for the find. As a small boy, he had somehow damaged this treasured family possession, and its repair had disclosed the hidden space. In it lay priceless letters written by Jefferson, Madison, Marshall, and Lafayette.

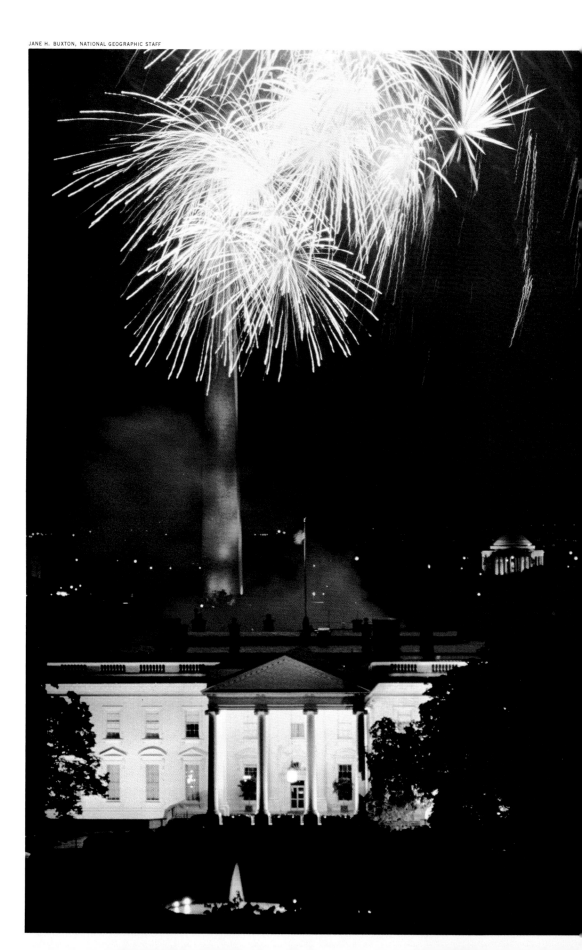

4

A HOUSE
FOR THE AGES

HE WAS THE PRESIDENT of the United States. He stood at the pinnacle of a political man's career. Yet he entered the White House without his wife and recently bereft of his only child to survive infancy; and on his inauguration night he slept in a house that was in utter disarray.

Such was the plight of Franklin Pierce on March 4, 1853. His personal life was filled with tragedy and bitterness; his wife had opposed his running for the Presidency, and she interpreted the death of their 11-year-old son Benjamin in a railway accident as a sacrifice demanded by God to leave her husband free to meet his national responsibilities. Mrs. Pierce did not arrive at the White House until later that month.

On the morning of what should have been his most triumphant day, President-elect Pierce had been escorted to the Capitol by the outgoing Chief Executive, Millard Fillmore. He delivered his inaugural address before a cheering crowd and rode to the White House, where for hours he accepted the congratulations of well-wishers.

It was growing late when the last of the handshakers departed, leaving behind soiled dishes and disarranged furniture. The servants had disappeared, and President Pierce and his private secretary, Sidney Webster, groped their way upstairs by candlelight to get what sleep they could before facing the problems of the new administration.

The chaotic conditions that met Franklin Pierce seem incredible now

Streamers of light etch the sky above the White House, lending color to drifts of smoke. The fireworks cannonade, synchronized to the music of Tchaikovsky's 1812 Overture, ended a picnic given for Members of Congress in May 1978.

in comparison with the smooth operation of the modern Executive Mansion. In Pierce's time, Presidents were expected to make their own living arrangements and to provide their own household help and supplies. Indeed, until the early 20th century the President had to pay for all of his and his family's daily needs, whether personal or in connection with official duties. He provided his own horses and carriages and was responsible for their upkeep.

To be sure, Congress appropriated money for repairs and furnishings for the mansion. To many people the annual presidential salary of $25,000 seemed enough to take care of everything else. But the appropriations often varied with the whims of Congress, and the cost of maintaining a household that reflected the dignity of the nation worked a hardship on many Presidents. Jefferson and Monroe later were forced to sell land to pay debts accumulated during their White House years.

Jefferson's numerous and lavish gourmet dinners—the result of a habit he acquired in France of "mitigating business with dinner"—virtually ate up his salary. In eight years his bills for wine alone came to nearly $11,000. And he once noted that when Congress was in session he needed a great deal more wine, especially champagne. Washington food costs were higher, too, than elsewhere. Jefferson's grocery bill often amounted to $50 a day—at a time when 75 cents for a turkey and $3 for a hog were considered high prices.

It was not until the Taft Administration that Congress relieved Presidents of having to pay the wages of house servants. Harding was the first President for whom the government picked up the check for official entertaining.

Congress also has recognized the advancing level of salaries in the U.S., though the sums paid the Chief Executive have lagged behind those received by many corporation presidents. In 1873, effective with Grant's second term, Congress raised the President's salary from $25,000 a year to $50,000. Taft, in 1909, became the first Chief Executive to earn $75,000; Truman, in 1949, was the first to receive $100,000. Since 1969, the annual salary has been $200,000.

President Franklin Pierce, candle in hand, leads his secretary upstairs in a dark, disordered White House after his inaugural reception in 1853. A troubled term followed this disheartening beginning.

The President, however, still must defray the First Family's living expenses. He pays for their food, laundry, and dry cleaning, for their personal telephone calls, and for all their private parties. President Clinton, for example, has footed the bill for his daughter, Chelsea, when she celebrated several birthdays at the White House, and for an array of other private parties for their friends.

Unlike President Pierce, the Chief Executive and First Lady who arrive at the White House today find a trained permanent staff ready to help manage what has now become a highly complex organization.

In many ways the house resembles a small, well-run hotel. Bed and table linens, glasses, silverware, and china—state and informal—are all provided. A storekeeper takes care of the daily marketing needs, and the Secret Service checks the purchases before delivery.

Back in William Henry Harrison's day, White House life was so casual that the President sometimes did his own marketing, carrying his groceries home in a basket. Mrs. Taft hired the first house-keeper in 1909, to supervise the food buying and the preparation of meals for both the President's family and guests. Previously a steward had seen to routine market-ing, and caterers met special requirements.

Each First Lady may make selections from furniture already in the mansion or from a government storehouse containing pieces used by previous tenants. And, of course, she may refurnish and redecorate the second- and third-floor quarters as she chooses.

The Ground Floor Corridor and principal public rooms on the first floor, however, will retain their museum character, in accordance with a law passed by Congress in 1961 to protect and continue the historical restoration begun by Mrs. Kennedy. Any proposed changes or addi-tions in these rooms must now be approved by the Com-mittee for the Preservation of the White House, established in 1964 by executive order.

In recent decades the President's wife has needed increasing help to keep her house presentable for the func-tions held there for the many and varied groups she is expected to entertain, and for the hundreds of thousands of visitors who tour the mansion.

The combined domestic and maintenance staffs—most of whom carry on from one administration to

Workmen hang a chandelier in the restored East Room during the 1948-52 reconstruction of the White House under President Harry Truman.

another—number about 90 employees: maids, laundresses, cooks, butlers, carpenters, painters, engineers, plumbers. At the head of these workers stands the chief usher; his job of coordinating the manifold activities cov-ers just about everything but ushering. If such a force seems large, con-sider how prodigious are the tasks, and how great the responsibility that goes with handling some of the nation's most valuable possessions. Con-sider, too, the normal wear and tear involved, and the cleaning, dusting, mopping, and polishing needed after more than 30,000 sightseers pass through the state rooms in a single week of the peak tourist season.

THE BIG KITCHEN opening off the arched Ground Floor Corridor is any chef's dream of equipment and working space. In this gleam-ing white and stainless-steel domain stand grinders, slicers, chop-pers, mixers, coffee roasters, electric ovens, and walk-in freezers. They help Executive Chef Walter Scheib and his assistants prepare state din-ners for as many as 180 guests, and hors d'oeuvres for 1,000 or more.

Such expert aid would have appeared nothing short of miraculous to those excellent housekeepers Abigail Adams and Dolley Madison.

In the second-floor President's Dining Room (right), David and Julie Nixon Eisenhower join her parents and sister, Tricia, for dinner. An 18th-century chandelier highlights the wallpaper, "The War of Independence." The first-floor Family Dining Room (below, as it looked in the 1890s) serves now chiefly for special occasions.

HARPER'S NEW MONTHLY MAGAZINE (BELOW); WHITE HOUSE PHOTOGRAPH

Mrs. Adams wrote to her sister that she would have been pleased to have had enough candles "lighting the apartments, from the kitchen to parlors and chambers...[and] wood enough to keep fires." Mrs. Madison "superintended all her domestic arrangements before breakfast," a biographer noted.

According to an admiring woman correspondent in the 1860s, a morning chore performed by capable Martha Patterson, daughter of President Andrew Johnson, was to "don a calico dress and spotless apron, and then descend to skim the milk and attend the dairy."

As recently as the Taft Administration, a cow named Pauline Wayne supplied milk for the household and grazed on the White House lawn.

Through the years, accounts of the latest home conveniences and comforts in the President's House have reflected the public interest in ever changing ways of life in the mansion.

The building Jefferson moved into in 1801 may have been "big enough for two emperors, one pope, and the grand lama," as a satirist observed, but it lacked practical arrangements for the everyday management of a home. So the President added colonnaded wings on either side of the mansion; they contained servants' quarters, workshops, an

In the gleaming White
House kitchen, Nancy
Reagan samples dishes
prepared by Roland
Mesnier (left), pastry
chef; Henry Haller, chief
chef (center); and cook
Frank Ruta. Mrs. Reagan
consulted with the chefs
before special events,
offering suggestions for
imaginative desserts such
as the spun-sugar
elephant and swan
creations on the table.
Below, pots, pans, and
pitchers line open shelves
in the White House
family kitchen of 1890.

icehouse, a meat house, a wine cellar, and a henhouse. Inside, the inventive Mr. Jefferson devised a series of revolving trays, called dumbwaiters, which he had built into the walls of his dining room, now the Family Dining Room. With this contrivance, guests could be served from outside the room without having waiters close enough to overhear their private conversations.

"You need not speak so low," Jefferson once assured a nervous guest. "Our walls have no ears."

PROBABLY THE GREATEST INCONVENIENCE of the early White House was the lack of running water. In the few months John and Abigail Adams lived there, servants had to haul water from nearly half a mile away. Jefferson set up an attic cistern with a system of wooden pipes reaching through the floors. But it was not until 1833, in Jackson's second term, that a system of iron pipes brought in spring water and permitted the old frontiersman to enjoy hot and cold showers.

Van Buren put in a basement "reservoir" with a "double-forcing pump" to supply water for kitchen and bathing needs. He thereby added fuel to the political fires stoked by Congressman Charles Ogle. In the "Gold Spoon" speech that accused the President of dining in decadent luxury, Ogle ridiculed him as one who indulged in the Grecian and Roman "pleasures of the warm or tepid bath...."

The precise date of the introduction of modern plumbing in the White House remains in doubt. But records show that in 1853 the family quarters had bathtubs with hot and cold running water. By 1876, water to several tubs and water closets was supplied by pipes connected to a 2,000-gallon tank in the attic.

The chronology of other improvements is clearer. In December 1848 the Polks became the first presidential couple to exchange oil lamps and candlelight for gas illumination. At a reception given soon after, the "brilliant jets suddenly vanished," leaving the guests in darkness—except in the Blue Room. There, Mrs. Polk said with satisfaction, she had had the foresight to retain the "elegant chandelier," whose "wax candles were shedding their soft radiance." President and Mrs. Fillmore introduced a kitchen stove in the 1850s, a newfangled contraption for the cook who had been preparing even the most lavish meals at a big, open fireplace filled with kettles, pots, skillets, hooks, and cranes.

From the start, the big rooms have been hard to heat. "Hell itself couldn't warm that corner," Jackson complained. The mansion's first central furnace—a coal-fueled, hot-water and hot-air system—was installed in 1853, after Franklin Pierce moved in.

President and Mrs. Benjamin Harrison introduced electric lighting but were timid about using it. Ike Hoover, who became chief usher during the Taft Administration, began his 42-year White House career in 1891 by setting up the novel system. He wrote later that the Harrisons "were afraid to turn the lights on and off for fear of getting a shock."

As each renovation and improvement brought in more wires, pipes,

A wide variety of people have always been needed to keep the White House operating. At top, Archie Roosevelt salutes as brother Quentin stands at ease during a roll call of the White House police. Bottom, from left to right: In the late 1800s, a houseman wields a feather duster; at the turn of the century, a messenger makes a delivery on horseback; today, volunteers help decorate the state rooms for Christmas.

and flues, walls and structural supports reflected the strain on the old house. The weird tappings and creakings that had bred ghost stories for years finally forced an engineering survey in 1948. The report disclosed that the structure "was standing up," as one investigator put it, "purely from habit." The alternatives: Reconstruct it or tear it down.

Backed by public pleas to save the White House, Congress provided funds to rip out the interior and restore it within the original shell. When the work was completed in 1952, the house at last was "built for ages to come," as Abigail Adams had seen it in 1800. It also was supplied with comforts that would have startled President Fillmore, who called it his "temple of inconveniences."

The big attic where Lincoln's and Theodore Roosevelt's children had played was transformed into a spacious bedroom annex for visiting friends and family. The Coolidges' "Sky Parlor," with its magnificent view to the south, became a solarium. Presidents and their wives, from the Eisenhowers on, have found this bright room a pleasant spot for informal entertaining, or a place to relax and read, to listen to music, or to watch television.

Children and adolescents have turned the room into a busy and happy place. Here was the Kennedy kindergarten; here Luci Johnson, surrounded by furniture she had painted, had her teenage hideaway. And here First Family youngsters have exchanged news and confidences with their friends.

The Carter family used the Solarium as a kind of second living room, more casual than the second-floor sitting halls. The Clintons give small get-togethers here amid comfortable, overstuffed sofas and chairs. The Solarium is also one of their favorite rooms for enjoying casual meals or watching television.

WORK ON THE WHITE HOUSE is never truly finished. Renovation of the exterior, begun during the Carter years, is finally nearing completion. It has included the removal of some 40 coats of paint, repairing of the stone, and repainting of much of the exterior. The Reagan years saw an improved security system and the addition of a special visitors' entrance. Outside this entrance, East Executive Avenue was transformed into a tree-lined pedestrian mall.

Of all the additions to the mansion's facilities, probably the most useful was the second-floor dining room, with its pantry and kitchen. By converting one of the bedroom suites of the second-floor apartment into a dining room and kitchen, the Kennedys made it possible for the family to enjoy meals with guests in a homelike atmosphere instead of having to use the State Dining Room or the smaller adjoining one on the formal first floor.

In this, the President's Dining Room, as it has been officially named, the blue-tone wallpaper depicts scenes of the American Revolution based on early 19th-century engravings. Studying the wallpaper during a small dinner in May 1981, Great Britain's Prince Charles good-naturedly chided

Workmen rebuild the interior of the White House on a framework of steel beams erected within the original shell. The complete renovation began in 1948, when President Truman noticed chandeliers swaying ominously. He ordered a study of the mansion, and a commission found it so weakened by years of alterations that the Trumans immediately moved across Pennsylvania Avenue to historic Blair House.

President Reagan for seating him where he had to look at Lord Cornwallis's surrender at Yorktown.

At one of the Nixons' dinner parties in this room, Alice Roosevelt Longworth surprised and amused her hosts and other guests when she suddenly exclaimed, "My goodness...this is the room where I had my appendix out."

The Bushes often dined alone or with guests in the President's Dining Room, but the Clintons prefer the less formal setting of the adjoining kitchen for family meals. They had its center island removed to accommodate a white table and rattan chairs, so that they could fix their own food, including "lots of leftovers," according to Mrs. Clinton.

Ongoing improvements to make the White House more energy efficient include the most extensive overhaul of the mansion's heating, ventilating, and air-conditioning system since the Truman Administration. Continuing efforts begun during the Bush Administration, the Clintons

As the renovation nears completion, carpenters (upper left) hang doors, and movers lug in furniture. Artisans (above) attach original moldings to a fireplace pillar. The Trumans moved back from Blair House in March 1952 after four years of work that cost $5,761,000.

have introduced energy-saving lighting throughout the building and grounds. A new refrigerator that uses half the energy of a standard one has been installed.

Mrs. Clinton has overseen the refurbishing of two of the formal spaces on the first floor of the White House—the Blue Room and the East Room. Worn, faded fabrics in the Blue Room were replaced with brilliant sapphire ones, while the walls were repapered in a gold pattern with a blue-and-gold swag border. The East Room, used for press conferences, bill signings, concerts, and receptions, had long been uncarpeted. Three pale green-and-gold woven rugs have been installed here to soften the appearance of the room and to provide better acoustics for special events. As part of the refurbishing, the mantels and baseboards have been stripped of faux-marble painting to reveal the original reddish-hued Vermont marble. It is all part of the continuous change that goes on in and around this house.

5

IN THE
PRESIDENT'S PARK

THE ROYALS' LIMOUSINE DROVE SLOWLY along the south lawn driveway to the White House. It was June 13, 1994, and Emperor Akihito and Empress Michiko of Japan were making a state visit to the President of the United States. The audience waited expectantly, each group in its assigned place: leading U.S. officials; a representative of the Diplomatic Corps; reporters; a battery of video and still photographers on a platform; and the public, admitted for the event.

As the Emperor and Empress and their party reached the Southwest Gate, President and Mrs. Clinton emerged from the Diplomatic Reception Room. The U.S. Army Herald Trumpets then played four "Ruffles and Flourishes" followed by "Hail to the Chief." When the visitors arrived at the White House, President and Mrs. Clinton came forward to shake their hands and to present Vice President and Mrs. Gore and other officials to them. The President escorted his guests along the traditional red carpet to the reviewing stand. The Herald Trumpets again played four "Ruffles and Flourishes." As a 21-gun salute was fired, the U.S. Marine Band played the Japanese national anthem, followed by the national anthem of the United States.

The Third U.S. Infantry, the historic Old Guard Fife and Drum Corps, trooped in review on the broad expanse of the south lawn. Then President Clinton officially welcomed the Emperor and Empress. The Emperor

To the tune of "Yankee Doodle," the Old Guard Fife and Drum Corps troops across the south lawn during the welcoming ceremony for Emperor Akihito of Japan on June 13, 1994. Moments earlier, batteries fired a 21-gun salute.

121

responded with a speech that reflected the ties between the two nations. Thus another foreign leader—the symbolic head of a nation that has become our peacetime ally and economic rival—had begun an official visit. The leading figures in the opening pageant could now attend a brief reception in the mansion and get on to official business.

THIS WELCOMING CEREMONY was first introduced by President Kennedy, and it has remained largely unchanged. In his time, it also included helicopter service to transport guests to the arrival rites. Johnson, Nixon, Ford, and Carter maintained the lift, though less frequently, but the practice has now come into disuse. Most state guests arrive in Washington the day before and are driven through the Southwest Gate to the meeting the next morning.

Helicopters, however, have become an important feature of presidential travel. Eisenhower was first to use them for trips to and from the White House. The choppers have continued to touch down on a pad near the South Entrance. They lift Presidents to nearby airfields, bring consultants to the mansion, and fly First Families to the Maryland retreat named Camp David for Eisenhower's grandson.

The helicopter flights and the state arrival ceremony, with its spectacular sound and color, have taken their place in the succession of historic acts presented on this outdoor stage for nearly two centuries.

Jefferson's Fourth of July celebrations included reviews of the District militia and other troops in the newly laid out "President's Park," with "their gay appearance and martial musick," wrote an eyewitness, "enlivening the scene, exhilerating the spirits of the throngs of people who poured in from the country and adjacent towns."

On April 10, 1865, jubilant crowds surged across the north lawn of the White House, singing and cheering over the news of Gen. Robert E. Lee's surrender at Appomattox. Soon President Lincoln came to a window in response to the cries of the people. He promised them he would make a victory speech later, but meantime he suggested that their enthusiastic band play "Dixie." It was one of the best tunes he had ever heard, he said, and he thought "we had fairly captured it."

The air age was young in 1911, when the broad south grounds of the White House witnessed a prophetic and dramatic sight. A pioneering pilot, Harry Nelson Atwood, landed there in a Burgess-Wright biplane soon after completing a record-setting cross-country flight, and President Taft presented him with a gold medal for the feat.

Over the years, the 18-acre estate that today surrounds the White House with well-kept gardens and lawns has shown different faces. John and Abigail Adams found it a barren expanse littered with workmen's shacks and tools. The grounds had appeared so grim before their arrival, in fact, that a member of the President's Cabinet wrote to one of the District Commissioners complaining that "a private gentleman preparing a residence for his Friend, would have done more than has been done." He suggested that the Commissioners plant "something like a garden,

"A most fitting addition to the White House," commented Leslie's in 1858 on Buchanan's new conservatory. The President's niece Harriet Lane walked here among her camellias to escape "the constant whirl of fashion." On public days visitors marveled at South American orange trees, aloes, and pitcher plants.

FRANK LESLIE'S ILLUSTRATED NEWSPAPER, TINTED BY P. HALL BAGLIE

at the North side of…[the] large, naked, ugly looking building….'' and provide a yard enclosure.

But it was President Jefferson who obtained funds to build the first fence. For a few years, this rustic rail-and-post enclosure blended nicely into a village capital where "Excellent snipe shooting and even partridge shooting was to be had on either side of the main avenue…,'' as the secretary of the British Legation noted. Then Jefferson replaced the wood fence with a fieldstone wall and constructed an imposing arched gate over the driveway leading to the entrance.

With his architect Benjamin Latrobe, Jefferson also devised an overall landscape plan. It included grading and planting the south grounds to provide more privacy, while leaving a central view toward the river.

It remained, however, for that austere New Englander and ardent gardener, John Quincy Adams, to devote the most lavish personal care of any President to the White House nurseries and gardens. In his diaries from 1825 to 1829 appear entries that tell of the happy hours he spent on this hobby. The accounts reveal his enjoyment of pungent herbs—balm, rue, sage, tansy, and tarragon—and his delight in the "deep blood-colored beet, the white-flowered carrot and yellow-flowered parsnip…."

In this "small garden, of less than two acres…," he wrote, there were "forest- and fruit-trees, shrubs, hedges, esculent vegetables, kitchen and medicinal herbs, hot-house plants, flowers and weeds, to the amount, I conjecture, of at least one thousand."

As had Jefferson, Adams planned to introduce useful crops to American farmers. On his rides about Washington and on travels to and from his Massachusetts home, he collected nuts, seeds, and seedlings, and encouraged his friends to do the same when they went abroad.

After Congress passed a resolution to encourage the growing of mulberry trees to form a base for a silkworm industry in the United States, Adams added the white mulberry to his flourishing White House nurseries. With his wife, Louisa, he nurtured silkworms on the leaves, and in the evenings he would sit beside her, writing, as she unreeled and rewound the fragile silk filaments from the cocoons.

Observing the havoc wrought by frost, searing sun, hailstorms, and insects on his precious growing things, the President remarked: "The infancy of plants seems to be as delicate as that of animals." He indulged in the hope, he confided to his diary, that a certain border of oaks, chestnuts, and other trees would "outlast many Presidents of the United States." Adams's dream of a silk industry never materialized. But one of his shade trees—a great American elm—survived until 1990, spreading its branches over the southeast lawn. In its place, Barbara Bush planted a new tree in 1991, one that had been propagated from the Adams elm.

WITH THE ARRIVAL of Andrew Jackson and the building of the North Portico that completed construction of the mansion, the evolution of the grounds entered a new phase. Instead of the rambling gardens of Adams, graveled footways appeared, along with a carriage house, driveway, and stable for the President's favorite racing horses. More lasting than either carriages or stable would be another Jackson innovation—a magnificent magnolia, in memory of his beloved Rachel, that still stands beside the South Portico.

As Washington grew less bucolic, the President's Park was enhanced with fountains and flower beds. In 1841, when Charles Dickens called to see President Tyler, he found the "ornamental ground about it…laid out in garden walks; they are pretty and agreeable to the eye; though they have that uncomfortable air of having been made yesterday…."

Time and professional landscape architects, including the talented Andrew Jackson Downing, would overcome the effect of newness that Dickens observed. Within 15 years, the White House estate, particularly its tree-dotted south lawn, had become part of "a scene of beauty and attractiveness…," according to an article in an 1856 issue of *United States Magazine*. Open to the public on weekdays, the "agreeable promenades" drew "the elite of the city," said the author. "Usually the President, the Cabinet, and the Foreign Ministers and their wives may be seen here [with] thousands of ladies and pretty children, most bewitchingly dressed…."

Stern-faced soldier for women's rights holds aloft her banner at the northwest corner of the White House grounds. During the Wilson Administration, before the Nineteenth Amendment gave women the vote, suffragettes picketed the White House, went on hunger strikes, and got themselves jailed. The President called their methods "unfortunate."

MR. PRESIDENT
HOW LONG
MUST
WOMEN WAIT
FOR LIBERTY

Microphone in hand, President
Wilson talks with a pilot circling
overhead in a demonstration of
air-ground communication on
November 22, 1918. Half a century
later, on July 21, 1969, television
captures an event witnessed by
millions across the globe: President
Nixon talks by radiotelephone
with the first men on the moon—
Apollo 11 Astronauts Neil A.
Armstrong and Edwin E. Aldrin, Jr.

For an added attraction on Saturday afternoons, the Marine Band played one of its lively concerts in what had long been a tradition of outdoor entertainment in the capital.

Around this time, President Buchanan's niece and official hostess, Harriet Lane, persuaded her uncle to build one of the greenhouses that would give much pleasure to future White House residents and visitors. In these steamy glass buildings, filled with the color and fragrance of exotic blossoms, fruits, and tangled tropical vines, Miss Lane became the first of many hostesses at the mansion to find a quiet haven away from the obligations of her official position.

Energetic Lucy Hayes worked there with trowel and shears among her lilies and roses. Frances Cleveland spent pleasant hours wandering with her girls along the sweet-scented aisles of the greenhouses. Caroline Harrison was fond of orchids. She had several rare varieties planted in the conservatory, and used the vivid, showy blooms as models for china she selected and painted. Mrs. Harrison also assembled pieces of White House china used by previous First Ladies. Out of her interest grew the White House china collection, which represents almost every presidential family.

From the time Buchanan's conservatories opened until they were torn down to make way for the West Wing, no First Lady had far to go for flowers or potted plants to decorate her home. Today, all flowers for arrangements come from wholesale distributors. Greenhouses of the National Park Service, which is responsible for the care and upkeep of the mansion and its grounds, supply potted plants.

The floral preferences of First Ladies make a varied bouquet. Mrs. Eisenhower, for example, showed a preference for sweetheart roses and carnations in her favorite color, pink. Mrs. Kennedy experimented with mixed floral designs, and Mrs. Johnson enjoyed each season's offerings—from spring pastels to deeper shades of fall. Mrs. Nixon took keen interest in planning floral colors and designs for state dinners. Mrs. Ford showed a definite preference for all kinds of lilies. And Mrs. Carter's choices followed the Kennedy style with simple garden flowers, such as roses and daisies.

Mrs. Reagan loved coral-colored arrangements in vermeil bowls. Mrs. Bush, who was an avid gardener, was especially fond of peonies, lilies, and all varieties of summer flowers.

The chief White House floral designer, Nancy Clarke, follows Mrs. Clinton's taste in flowers for the house. The First Lady favors contemporary arrangements of warm-colored red and yellow flowers, as well as those using a variety of garden flowers. Among her favorites is a cream-hued rose with a red edge, called candia. Ms. Clarke and her staff arrange flowers for the public areas of the White House visible during tours and for the private quarters upstairs. On formal occasions, her arrangements are scattered throughout the White House, and outside, too, when an event takes place under a tent.

Beginning with Woodrow Wilson, all the Presidents, and some of their wives, have planted trees on the White House grounds, known as the President's Park. Jimmy Carter brought a red maple from his Georgia farm. He knew all the old trees by name and took a special interest in their care. Ronald Reagan planted three trees, the Bushes, five.

President and Mrs. Clinton have carried on the tree-planting tradition, adding more than half a dozen to the park, including a white dogwood planted in memory of the children who died in the April 1995 bombing of the federal building in Oklahoma City.

Many Presidents have set up recreational facilities on the grounds. Hayes marked off a croquet court near the South Portico, where, a staff member wrote, clerks as well as the family "used to spend an hour now and then…over hard-fought games with mallet and ball."

There has been a tennis court on the south lawn since the time of Theodore Roosevelt. The press called associates who joined him for a fast, tough game his "tennis Cabinet." Harding practiced his golf shots on the lawn and trained his Airedale, Laddie Boy, to retrieve the balls. Hoover exercised with his "medicine-ball Cabinet" before breakfast conferences under the magnolias. Truman pitched horseshoes; Eisenhower improved his golf on a presidential putting green.

Ford installed the first outdoor swimming pool, near the Oval Office. The Carter family enjoyed the pool, the tennis courts, and the bowling alley under the North Portico. President Reagan had no opportunity to enjoy his favorite exercise, horseback riding, on the White House grounds. Both he and the First Lady used exercise equipment installed in a second-floor room. Reagan worked out here more frequently during his recovery from an assassination attempt.

George Bush, a very active President, added a horseshoe pit and a basketball half-court, and pursued jogging, golf, tennis, and swimming. During the Clinton Administration, a quarter-mile jogging track was added, and the Eisenhower putting green was restored on the south grounds.

For relaxation and fitness, Presidents turn to sports. George Bush pitched horseshoes, as did Harry Truman

CHILDREN PARTICULARLY have found the rolling acres of the south lawn a great playground. Here they can explore hidden nooks in hedges and bushes, ride ponies, and raise pets of every description. Little Tad Lincoln made a pet of a turkey that relatives sent for the family's Christmas dinner in 1863. He named it Jack. When the cook prepared to kill the turkey, Tad ran in tears to his father, who interrupted a Cabinet meeting to write an official reprieve.

Another President's son faced a less amenable father. T.R. once caught young Quentin walking on stilts through a flower bed. The boy obeyed Roosevelt's stern order to get out of the flowers, but grumbled, "I don't see what good it does *me* for you to be President."

Once a year—on Easter Monday—Washington youngsters are invited to an egg-rolling party on the south grounds. This is one of the last events at the President's House still open to the public. In 1879 this event, which had been held on the Capitol grounds for many years, was moved to the White House on the invitation of President Hayes.

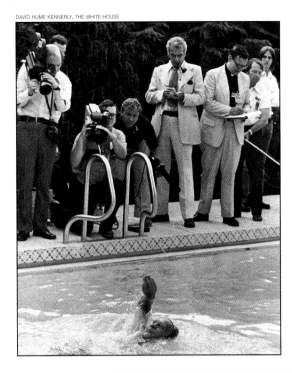

*(above). Gerald Ford enjoyed swimming.
Bill Clinton prefers jogging. Here, he
runs beside President Kim Young Sam of
South Korea and his aides on the new
quarter-mile White House track.*

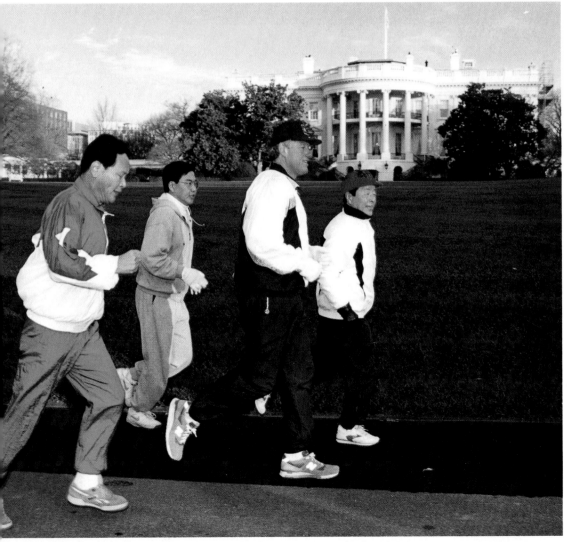

Some 28,000 children and parents waited for hours to flock through the gates for the White House Easter Egg Roll of April 12, 1993. On the South Portico the Marine Band played a medley of tunes. Magicians, jugglers, wrestlers, bands, and the folksingers Peter, Paul, and Mary provided entertainment on the south lawn and the Ellipse. A petting zoo had bunnies and a horse. A large bald eagle, on loan from a wildlife hospital, impressed children and adults.

President Clinton, attending with the First Lady (official hostess of the event), blew a whistle to start a round of the egg rolling. The object is to see how fast a child can move a hard-boiled egg across a grassy slope with a spoon. All of the participants were declared winners; each took home as a souvenir a wooden egg bearing the signatures of the Clintons.

Many children hunted among a pile of straw for the eggs, which bore, in some cases, the pawprint signature of Socks, the First Cat. Other eggs were signed by famous people, such as Barbra Streisand, Dan Marino, Mister Rogers, and recent astronauts. As always, giant Easter bunnies wandered the grounds as cheerful mascots for the occasion.

Whatever the event, few settings could be lovelier than the rolling expanse of lawn as viewed from the balcony added to the South Portico during the Truman Administration. Looking past a shimmering pool and fountains toward the Washington Monument and Jefferson Memorial, a visitor today would find it hard to realize that this area once merged with malarial marshes along a creek, which by 1817 had been walled and deepened into a sluggish canal. Odorous with sewage, garbage, and dead animals, alive with mosquitoes and flies, the canal was the bane of White House occupants.

As a summer retreat, Van Buren rented a house in nearby Georgetown. Buchanan and Lincoln were glad to go back and forth in hot months to a cottage lent them at the Soldiers' Home three miles away. "I am alone in the White pest-house," a Lincoln secretary wrote a friend. "The ghosts of twenty thousand drowned cats come in at night through the south windows." In 1872 the canal-sewer was covered and the street it created was named Constitution Avenue. With filling and landscaping, the present Ellipse was completed by 1884. Future Presidents could graciously entertain outdoors.

THE THEODORE ROOSEVELTS started the trend with a series of lawn parties, inviting Cabinet members and other friends. When President and Mrs. Taft celebrated their silver anniversary in June 1911, they received more than 3,000 guests on the south grounds, where trees and bushes sparkled with tiny, colored lights, and strings of paper lanterns cast shadows on the lawn. Mrs. Taft later wrote happily of the occasion that "a more brilliant throng was never gathered in this country." In the summer of 1918, President and Mrs. Wilson began inviting war veterans to attend an annual garden fete.

Summer after summer, the south lawn has offered a perfect setting for large gatherings. The Eisenhowers, for example, held a reception

Racing and tumbling down a hillock, children romp on the south lawn during the 1887 Easter Monday egg rolling. More than a century later (right), on April 12, 1993, the Clintons' first Easter Egg Roll drew a high-spirited crowd for what has become the largest public event at the White House each year. The President enjoyed shaking hands with the participants.

there for more than 4,000 members of the American Bar Association and counselors from the British Commonwealth.

The Kennedy children shared their playground with 1,700 youngsters from child-care agencies when the kilted Black Watch—the Royal Highland Regiment—paraded to the skirl of bagpipes.

On a huge stage erected on the south lawn, President Johnson presented awards to outstanding high-school graduates who had won a place in his annual Presidential-Scholar program, begun in 1964.

In a Rose Garden reception on September 24, 1981, President Reagan honored Sandra Day O'Connor—the first woman to be named to the U.S. Supreme Court. And President Bush also held numerous official events in the Rose Garden, including a meeting with the Cincinnati Reds, after their triumphant victory in the 1990 World Series.

President and Mrs. Clinton, like their predecessors, make good use of the Rose Garden. Here, the President has held press conferences and signed such historic legislation as the Family Leave Bill in February 1993. The garden has been the site for the official swearing-in of various officials, including Louis J. Freeh as head of the FBI, whose initiation ceremony took place on a warm, sunny day in July 1993.

On a lighter note, the Rose Garden formed the backdrop for the May 1994 wedding of Mrs. Clinton's brother Anthony Rodham to Nicole Boxer. This marked the first White House nuptials since Tricia Nixon's marriage nearly 23 years earlier.

Each year the President also accepts a Thanksgiving turkey, presented by the National Turkey Federation, in the Rose Garden. In 1994 the honored bird was a 50-pounder named Tom, from Harrisonburg, Virginia, who tried to flee from all the hoopla before President Clinton had emerged from the Oval Office. His handlers recaptured him and placed him back atop the green-draped presentation table, where, a bit dazed, he endured his brief moment of fame without further incident. Tom, like his predecessors in recent years, evaded the roasting pan to live out his days as a tourist attraction at a nearby farm park.

ON THE SOUTH LAWN, other gatherings and receptions come and go in colorful procession. In June 1993, President and Mrs. Clinton held a barbecue for more than a thousand journalists. Guests enjoyed badminton, volleyball, and a comic amateur musical revue by the White House communications staff.

The tradition of an annual picnic for Members of Congress, held each year on the south lawn, has been kept up by Bill and Hillary Clinton. On June 23, 1994, about 1,000 attended the Congressional Crab Feast, where they enjoyed crab salad and hard-shell crabs, as well as entertainment by country vocalist Trisha Yearwood.

Perhaps the most stirring moment of the Clinton Presidency occurred on September 13, 1993. In front of 3,000 guests, including former Presidents Bush and Carter, two longtime foes, Israeli Prime Minister Yitzhak Rabin and Palestine Liberation Organization Chairman Yasser

The President's Park has always been a wonderful place for children. Above, white-frocked girls dance around a maypole during Hoover's tenure. Right, cedar boughs shade Amy Carter's tree house, also a favorite perch for her nephew Jason. Below, Franklin Roosevelt's grandchildren "Sistie" and "Buzzie" take advantage of a new-fallen snow in December 1939, pelting each other with powdery balls.

A President often has to pause and take time out of a busy schedule for important ceremonial events. Opposite: In April 1993, the Clintons, accompanied by Vice President and Mrs. Gore, head for a party on the south lawn for White House volunteers. The President paid tribute to people who had freely given of their time in a variety of capacities. Two years later, President and Mrs. Clinton plant a dogwood tree on the White House grounds (below) in memory of the children killed in the bombing of the Oklahoma City federal building.

Arafat, shook hands after the signing of a framework for peace. Citing the years of war between the Arabs and Jews over Palestine, the President spoke of their agreement as an "extraordinary act in one of history's defining dramas." He went on to assert that "…this bold new venture today, this brave gamble that the future can be better than the past must endure…."

A year later, a tent set up on the soggy south lawn was the scene for a celebration honoring writers and composers of music. White House pastry chef Roland Mesnier had prepared chocolate truffles, chocolate-dipped strawberries, lemon white-chocolate mousse, and pecan cookies for the 1,200 guests. Performances by Michael Bolton, the Pointer Sisters, and Ruth Brown, among others, highlighted the evening.

But wherever the President goes, his office goes with him. For his work is never done, whether he is editing a speech aboard his speeding plane or reading the latest of his daily reports at midnight in his study or his bedroom.

6

THE LONELIEST PLACE

"NO EASY MATTER will ever come to you…," said President Eisenhower to President-elect Kennedy on the eve of the 1961 inauguration. "If they're easy they will be settled at a lower level."

President Taft called the White House "the loneliest place in the world." After one year in office, Theodore Roosevelt wrote: "Everyday, almost every hour, I have to decide very big as well as very little questions, and…what it is possible…to achieve." On President Truman's desk stood a sign that read "The buck stops here." Bill Clinton described the responsibilities of office more optimistically, noting that "with all of its troubles and difficulties, every day is still an exhilarating opportunity to serve and make a difference."

As the representative of all the people, the President must balance the often-conflicting interests of many groups and sections in seeking the common good. Yet he can never forget that the individual American also looks directly to him as the holder of the office that—in Herbert Hoover's words—"touches the happiness of every home."

Seldom, if ever, can the Chief Executive escape the pressures of his job, whether engaging in a favorite sport or relaxing in the intimacy of his family circle. To all, friends or strangers, he has suddenly become a man whose magic words can unlock the gifts of position and wealth. His election has given him powers that in scope and variety are unique. He is at

Unrelenting paperwork keeps outdoorsman Theodore Roosevelt at his desk. He later wrote of the "incredible amount of administrative work with which the President has to deal even in time of peace. He is of necessity a very busy man."

CENTURY MAGAZINE, MARCH 1897 (BELOW); JUDGE, MARCH 23, 1889, BOTH LIBRARY OF CONGRESS once the ceremonial head of government, leader of a political party, administrator of the nation's laws and domestic affairs, director of foreign policy, and Commander in Chief of the Armed Forces.

How this many-faceted power has been used has depended on the era, the character, and the conscience of each President, for the Constitution laid out few specific guidelines for the conduct of the office. As Woodrow Wilson put it, the President is "at liberty…to be as big a man as he can. His capacity will set the limit…."

In 1800, when the country was young and weak, John Adams took the initiative in ending an undeclared naval war with France over the sensitive issue of freedom of the seas for United States shipping.

The war then raging between France and Great Britain had led French privateers to seize American merchantmen, and open hostilities broke out. Adams, who at first had been as belligerent as many of his countrymen, turned to efforts at conciliation. When he learned that France was ready to discuss terms, he defied opposition and sent negotiators to Paris, and was so proud of their success that he once suggested having his tombstone record his part in making peace.

Madison faced a far more painful decision in the War of 1812—called "Madison's War" by his foes. Again the quarrel was over freedom of the seas during a war between England and France. But this time Napoleon pretended to respect the United States' neutrality, thus intensifying the outcries against the British for preying on American ships.

Swayed by that fact, and prodded by the "War Hawks" of the West who dreamed of annexing Canada, Madison pressed Congress for a declaration of war against Britain. But at the darkest hour of the conflict, when Dolley Madison and the Cabinet were in flight from the burning capital, the President must have wondered if he had endangered all that the Revolution had won.

Outgoing President Grover Cleveland leaves successor Benjamin Harrison holding the door in a cartoon deriding the seemingly endless flow of office seekers demanding the Chief Executive's time. At left, applications and recommendations cover the desk as Cleveland and Postmaster General William Lyne Wilson work far into the night appointing postmasters.

THE CONCLUSION of the War of 1812 permitted the nation to look westward again. Surprisingly, the greatest territorial expansion after the Louisiana Purchase was gained by a President seldom mentioned today. In 1844 James K. Polk was a dark-horse candidate, yet he became a strong leader whose policies fixed the western border of the United States along the shores of the Pacific Ocean.

As a follower and protégé of Jackson, Polk was well nicknamed "Young Hickory." Elected as a frank expansionist, he succeeded in bringing most of the present-day Southwest into the Union—though at the cost of an unpopular war with Mexico—and in acquiring the Oregon country north to the 49th parallel by a compromise with Britain. Still quoted today is the catchy slogan, "54-40 or fight," used by Polk's militant followers in demanding the northernmost boundary of the Oregon territory. Yet Polk's own shrewd diplomatic maneuvers that averted a third war with Great Britain have generally been forgotten.

When formulating and promoting policies, most Presidents have shown a high regard for the people's support and understanding. "I shall go just so fast and only so fast as I think I'm right and the people are ready for the step," said Lincoln. Benjamin Harrison declared that public opinion was "the most potent monarch this world knows."

Indeed, public opinion often may weigh more heavily in a President's decision than advice from his Cabinet. Chief Executives have varied sharply in consulting Cabinet members on important matters—a choice left open by the Constitution. Monroe conferred at length with his Cabinet, and especially with Secretary of State John Quincy Adams, before pronouncing the Monroe Doctrine that warned European powers against further expansion in the Western Hemisphere.

On the other hand, Jackson largely bypassed his Cabinet, preferring to discuss issues with friends, who were disparaged as his "kitchen Cabinet" but who served him capably and loyally.

Even during the first and second World Wars, Presidents Wilson and Roosevelt seldom called a Cabinet session. Roosevelt, like Jackson, chose to confer with outsiders of differing views, and with some of his administrative assistants whose qualifications, he said, were "high competence, great physical vigor, and a passion for anonymity."

Fortunately the Chief Executive does not always face world-shaking decisions. His day-to-day duties, however, are with him always, and have steadily increased. John Adams complained that a "peck of troubles in a large bundle of papers...comes every day...there is no pleasure."

When John Quincy Adams, in turn, took on the Presidency, the growing paperwork was made almost unbearable by his failure to delegate it. To cope with the minutiae, he used shorthand no one else could decipher, and impaired his eyesight and health by

Edith Wilson, who married the widower President in 1915, assists her husband.

writing thousands of words a week in official and personal correspondence. James K. Polk was similarly inclined. "No President who performs his duty faithfully...can have any leisure," he declared. "If he entrusts the details...to subordinates constant errors will occur. I prefer to supervise the whole operation of the Government myself...."

Already, however, this had become impossible. Polk's attempt to do the task put such a strain on his frail constitution that he became ill and died at age 53, a few months after leaving office.

Congress, too, was slow to provide funds for executive help. Most early Presidents called on a relative to act as private secretary, paying salaries from their own pockets. Congress finally voted money to hire one private secretary for President Buchanan; then the Civil War suddenly increased the need.

Lincoln acquired two bright and talented young secretaries, John Hay and John Nicolay. But no one could shield the President from the burdens of a country at war, nor would he permit himself to be sheltered from the avalanche of problems unloaded by officials, generals, war contractors, cranks, wounded soldiers, and tearful wives and mothers.

Most annoying was the clamor of petitioners for public office, often raised by those without qualifications. Lincoln told of a man who asked for a post as a foreign minister and gradually reduced his demands until he was willing to settle for an old pair of pants. Office seekers, however, had become pests long before Lincoln's Administration. They and their eager sponsors haunted the White House even in the time of John Adams. Jackson openly used the spoils system to reward his supporters. For a time fear stalked the ranks of his opponents in government service; in all, it is estimated, about one-fifth of the entire workforce was replaced.

With each change of administration came fresh hordes of office seekers. During William Henry Harrison's tenure, a group of men once barred him from a Cabinet meeting until he accepted their applications. President after President complained of the persecution and senseless waste of time. Yet it was not until after Garfield's murder by a thwarted job hunter that firm action was taken. In 1883 Congress passed the Pendleton Act, the first major reform law to open the way to competitive examinations as the basis for most federal service.

The nation was coming of age. Such changes in public attitude toward the obligations and rights of the man in the White House reflected the increasing energy, wealth, and population of the country.

Twentieth-century Presidents, supervising the nerve center of action in the West Wing, have found that the pace of their work has grown ever faster with new technology.

President Franklin D. Roosevelt signs the Social Security Act, August 14, 1935.

Theodore Roosevelt carried out his dynamic foreign and domestic programs in a period when messengers on horseback or bicycle rushed urgent letters and documents between the White House, Congress, and executive departments. Automobiles came in with Taft. Harding was the first President to broadcast a speech by radio, Truman the first to deliver an address from the White House by television. The first airplane assigned to the Chief Executive was a specially built C-54 used once by Franklin Roosevelt, and later by Truman. Jets and helicopters have been supplied since Eisenhower's time.

B ACK IN 1877 President Hayes installed a telephone at the mansion after seeing one demonstrated by inventor Alexander Graham Bell. Yet as late as Taft's term only one operator was needed to handle calls. When the operator went to lunch, young Charlie Taft considered it great sport to take over the switchboard. Today 16 telephone operators routinely take an average of 5,000 calls a day—and thousands more at times of national stress.

Gone are the days when Cleveland could write many of his letters and speeches by hand, or when McKinley and his staff of a dozen people could cope with all of the business. Wilson sometimes picked up a letter from a secretary's desk and answered it on his own typewriter. Harding was the first President to hire a professional speechwriter.

As the problems have increased and grown more complex, the presidential staff has come to include secretaries, consultants, and aides at the White House, plus economic, technical, and other advisory groups in the neighboring Executive Office Buildings.

To their regular schedules, Presidents in this century have added travels abroad. T.R. was the first to leave the United States, when he went to Panama in 1906. Wilson pioneered in going to Europe after World War I; FDR was first to visit South America and Hawaii, and he attended the historic World War II conferences at Casablanca, Tehran, and Yalta. Truman went to Germany for the famous Potsdam Conference held just before the war's end.

Since then every Chief Executive has traveled widely. Johnson was the first to fly around the world on state visits. Nixon also circled the globe, and in 1972 he became the first American head of state to visit the People's Republic of China. Ford met with world leaders in Japan, Korea, and Soviet Asia, as well as in many European countries. And Carter matched all previous records when he and, at times, his wife—as his personal representative—traveled to nations in Europe, the Middle East, Africa, Latin America, and the Caribbean.

During his Presidency, Ronald Reagan traveled around the world to meet with foreign leaders. In London in 1982, he gave the first address ever made by an American President to both Houses of Parliament. He also traveled to confer with Soviet leader Mikhail Gorbachev twice, once in Geneva in 1985 and again in Reykjavik, Iceland, in 1986.

George Bush traveled widely while President, making several trips to Europe in 1989 and 1990 to meet with NATO representatives, with further official visits to Japan, the Soviet Union, the Middle East, and Africa.

President Clinton's travel schedule has been full as well. In July 1993, he attended the Group of Seven economic summit in Tokyo and traveled to Korea, where he confirmed that "the United States intends to remain actively engaged in this region." On his first European trip, in January 1994, he participated in a NATO summit in Brussels and met with leaders of state in Prague, Minsk, and Moscow. Six months later, he returned to Europe for ceremonies marking the 50th anniversary of the D-Day invasion, a time when, Clinton said, "the sheer will of freedom's forces changed the course of this century." Fall 1994 saw him pursuing peace initiatives in the Middle East and attending an economic conference in Indonesia.

Early in 1995 President Clinton paid a goodwill visit to Canada, and later in the spring went to Haiti to help celebrate the role of U.S. troops in restoring democracy there. In December he became the first U.S. President to visit Northern Ireland, where he was warmly greeted by Catholic and Protestant residents. He met with political leaders of all factions, encouraging them to "stand firm against terror." In April 1996 the President and First Lady visited Japan. He and Prime Minister Hashimoto signed a declaration endorsing U.S. military presence in the Asia-Pacific region "as essential for preserving peace and stability."

N OTHING BETTER ILLUSTRATES the interest in the President's activities than does the news coverage that follows him wherever he goes. Teams of reporters accompany him on travels, check his daily appointments, and quiz him on policy at press conferences.

As an institution, the press conference began when President Wilson initiated formal question-and-answer meetings with reporters to explain his programs. It has continued in varied forms, from requiring reporters to submit written queries to the present rapid-fire questioning under television lights. Originally held in the Oval Office, the conferences were moved to the Old Executive Office Building during the Eisenhower Administration. Now they usually occur in the East Room or West Wing.

Press accommodations have come a long way since reporters had to pick up what news crumbs they could from outside the mansion's entrance. Theodore Roosevelt provided the first White House newsroom in his new West Wing, reputedly after taking pity on reporters shivering in a winter storm. Further improvements were made in 1970, when a press center was built over Franklin Roosevelt's swimming pool. It includes a

First official White House fleet of horseless carriages lines up in front of the garage—the former stable. William Howard Taft, in 1909, ordered (from left) a White steamer, a Baker electric, and two Pierce Arrows.

Harry Doll, George Augur, Gracie Doll.   *Chiefs of the Sioux nation and President Calvin Coolidge.*

Callers from many worlds have found hospitality at the White House. In 1874 King Kalakaua of the Sandwich Islands (now Hawaii) visited Ulysses S. Grant. Harding greeted a circus giant and two midget friends, as well as movie stars Dorothy and Lillian Gish, producer D. W. Griffith, and evangelist Billy Sunday. Coolidge's impassive expression rivaled those of Sioux chiefs visiting in 1925. Hoover presented the National Geographic Society's Gold Medal to Amelia Earhart after her solo Atlantic flight. After his talk with Eisenhower, Prince Faisal stepped onto the snowy grounds in his flowing desert robes. Johnson and Hubert Humphrey pause during their stroll on the lawn to greet sightseers at the Southeast Gate. In 1979 Jimmy and Rosalynn Carter welcomed Pope John Paul II, the first Pontiff to meet with a President in the mansion.

President and Mrs. Carter with Pope John Paul II.

Prince Faisal of Saudi Arabia.   *President Eisenhower greeting Indian Prime Minister Jawaharlal Nehru.*

King David Kalakaua.

Dorothy Gish, David Wark Griffith, Lillian Gish.

Evangelist Billy Sunday.

President Johnson and Vice President Humphrey shaking hands with tourists.

Truman with General de Gaulle.

Diana Hopkins, Winston Churchill.

Hoover and Amelia Earhart.

briefing room and two floors of booths for writers and broadcasters.

The news media follow the President's wife with equal scrutiny, and each First Lady plays an important role in her own way. Back in John Adams's time, critics felt that witty, politically sophisticated Abigail had too much influence on the President. To one of them she was *"her* Majesty" and "Mrs. President."

Throughout the 19th century most wives avoided a political role, limiting themselves to charity and to mild support of such broad issues as temperance and women's suffrage. Dolley Madison helped found and direct a capital orphanage, and was said to have contributed "$20 and a cow" to it. Sarah Polk worked as the President's private secretary, clipping and summarizing war news and political reports for him. Edith Wilson protected her ill husband by screening his visitors and official papers so persistently that critics called her "Mrs. President," too.

But the first wife of a President to participate actively in national affairs was Eleanor Roosevelt. She offered the first press conferences for newswomen, and produced prime news during the sessions. She traveled so much on lectures, visits to overseas troops, and as the "eyes and ears" of FDR that her White House code name was "Rover."

Lady Bird Johnson turned out to be another "Woman Doer," to use the title she created to honor outstanding women, including those active in her own programs to beautify the landscape and to give needy children a preschool boost to education through "Head Start." Patricia Nixon became a goodwill ambassador to Latin America in 1970. After an earthquake shook a vast area of Peru, she flew into the devastated region in a cargo plane carrying emergency supplies.

Betty Ford, with her personal warmth and interest in people, made friends for her husband and for her country as she traveled with him at home and abroad. She gave strong support to women's issues and the

"The war . . . is coming very close to home," FDR *warns in a radio broadcast on May 27, 1941, less than seven months before the Japanese attack on Pearl Harbor. The President invited representatives of 20 American republics and Canada to hear his address in the East Room.*

performing arts. Rosalynn Carter embarked on many far-reaching programs, including a national drive that she initiated and led to improve
the care of America's mentally ill. Nancy Reagan worked hard to fight
drug abuse among children and held conferences to support drives to combat the problem. Barbara Bush devoted much time to promoting literacy.

Hillary Rodham Clinton has redefined the traditional First Lady's
role, becoming more publicly active in policy matters than most of her
predecessors. In January 1993 she became head of the Task Force on
National Health Care Reform, which sought to forge a new health care
system for the country that would help contain costs and extend health
insurance to more people. The plan failed to meet with congressional
approval. However, despite the health care defeat, the First Lady remains
actively involved in her husband's Presidency, speaking out on behalf of
women, children, and health issues. Mrs. Clinton has also fostered an
appreciation of contemporary American cuisine, crafts, and sculpture,
using the White House as a showcase.

Yet, despite all the support a President may receive from his wife and
from his advisers, nothing can relieve him of the sole responsibility of making the nation's ultimate decisions. With word and act, he marks his place
in history when he signs or vetoes a bill on economic affairs, for instance;
when he proposes a foreign-aid program; or issues an executive order for
military operations abroad.

The more forceful the President, the more distinct his image. Cartoons
of Teddy Roosevelt, for one, with his toothy grin and round glasses, evoke
the earnest conservationist who helped preserve the nation's natural
resources, and the indomitable David who fought the Goliaths of indus-
trial monopoly.

The weight of the President's obligations is never so starkly displayed, however, as when his decision alone sets his country on a path of

*Beneath the glare of
television lights,
President Clinton
expounds on a point to
journalists gathered in
the Roosevelt Room on
the eve of a trip to Japan
and South Korea in July
1993. The trip proved a
success and highlighted
the importance of
presidential diplomacy.*

life or death, peace or war. Facing such a challenge, McKinley wept, said a confidant, in pouring out his troubles in the Red Room during the frantic days before the Spanish-American War. Wilson's call for a declaration of war against Germany followed sleepless nights of assessing the consequences. After Truman took the awesome responsibility of the atomic bombing of Japan in World War II, he wrote in his autobiography that he "regarded the bomb as a military weapon and never had any doubt that it should be used."

As the weapons of war grew ever more nightmarish, there came the perilous week in 1962 when the United States and the Soviet Union stood "eyeball to eyeball," H-bombs ready. President Kennedy had made his irrevocable decision to block Soviet ships from bringing more ballistic missiles to Cuba. Until the Soviet Union backed off, the world's future wavered in the balance.

TEN YEARS LATER, an unprecedented domestic crisis cast its first dark shadow across the Nixon White House with news of a break-in at the offices of the Democratic National Committee in the capital. Linked with the Republican Committee to Re-elect the President, the seemingly minor incident grew into a series of investigations and criminal indictments that resulted in President Nixon's resignation in the face of almost certain impeachment.

Though such moments of high drama are mercifully rare in White House history, every President deals from time to time with international tensions. Early in September 1978 Jimmy Carter initiated a series of meetings at Camp David that brought together President Sadat of Egypt and Prime Minister Begin of Israel. As a result of intense three-way discussions, Carter achieved a history-making accord between the two countries. Ronald Reagan found the tinderbox in the Middle East and terrorism elsewhere in the world continuing threats to peace. However, two summit meetings with Soviet leader Gorbachev initiated a useful dialogue on arms limitation and nuclear proliferation.

One of George Bush's biggest achievements was his facing down of Iraqi aggression in 1991. He sent American troops to the Middle East to force the retreat of Saddam Hussein's forces from Kuwait in an action known as Operation Desert Storm. Yet peace in this area remains elusive.

Presidents continue to wrestle not just with overseas challenges, but with domestic issues too. The Clinton Administration focused considerable energy on addressing some of these issues. In an effort to help the working poor, the administration expanded the earned income tax credit. Clinton also undertook social legislation in the field of education, including increased funding for the Head Start program for children. His health care reform package, aimed at lowering medical costs and providing widespread health insurance to Americans, failed to move through Congress. However, the President was able to get stiffer gun control and crime prevention measures legislated.

Beyond our borders, an equally complex world continues to challenge

With President Clinton's beaming encouragement, Israeli Prime Minister Yitzhak Rabin and PLO Chairman Yasser Arafat reach across the divide of decades of enmity to shake hands after the signing of a historic peace agreement on September 13, 1993. About 3,000 guests attended the emotion-filled ceremony held on the south lawn of the White House.

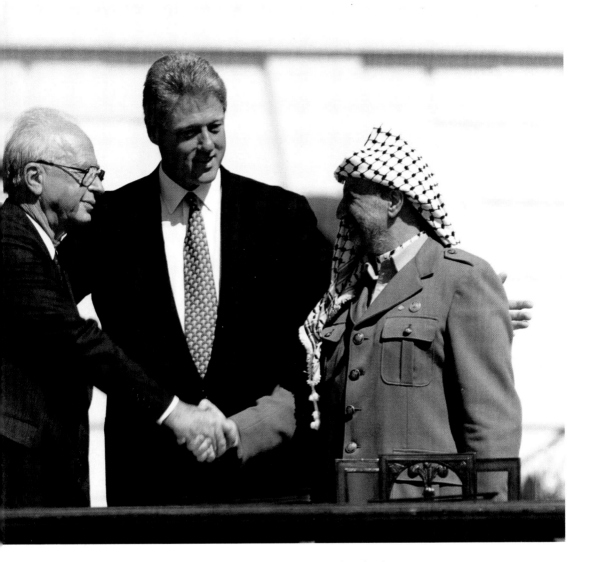

those who call the White House home. To open up international trade, the North American Free Trade Agreement (NAFTA) and the General Agreement on Tariffs and Trade (GATT) were signed into law during the Clinton Administration.

Elsewhere around the globe, the United States has remained a key player, helping to restore democracy to Haiti, negotiating a nuclear arms freeze with Ukraine and Belarus, and brokering peace agreements between Israel and both the PLO and Jordan.

Solutions to wars and economic problems will always be hard to find. However, between the great events of crisis and celebration, most Americans tend to regard their White House as a serene place—one that is usually glamorous and yet always attainable by an ambitious citizen.

On one occasion, a visitor ended a public tour of the mansion in company with a boy about nine years old. The boy, she reported, looked back at the big white building shining in the sun.

"I'm going to live here," he said confidently, "when I grow up."

INDEX

Boldface indicates illustrations; *italic* refers to picture legends (captions).

THE LIVING WHITE HOUSE printed and bound by R. R. Donnelley & Sons Co., Willard, Ohio. Cover and dust jacket printed by Southeastern Color Graphics, Johnson City, Tenn.